PAM GEMS

Plays Seven

PAM GEMS

Plays Seven

THE ODD WOMEN

THE AMIABLE COURTSHIP OF
MIZ VENUS AND WILD BILL

DARLING BOY

CEDRIC AND LOUISE

MY WARREN

Q

QUOTA BOOKS LTD
LONDON

Published in 2022 by Quota Books Ltd.
197 Hammersmith Grove, London W6 0NP
website: www.quotabooks.com – email: info@quotabooks.com
Twitter: @Quotabooks

A CIP record for this book is available from the British Library.

ISBN 978-1-7398894-2-5

Typeset in the UK by M Rules
Printed and bound by Biddles
Picture of Pam Gems courtesy of Jonathan Gems
Cover by TRISTAN

Available from Amazon, Ingram Spark, Quota Books
and all politically correct bookstores.

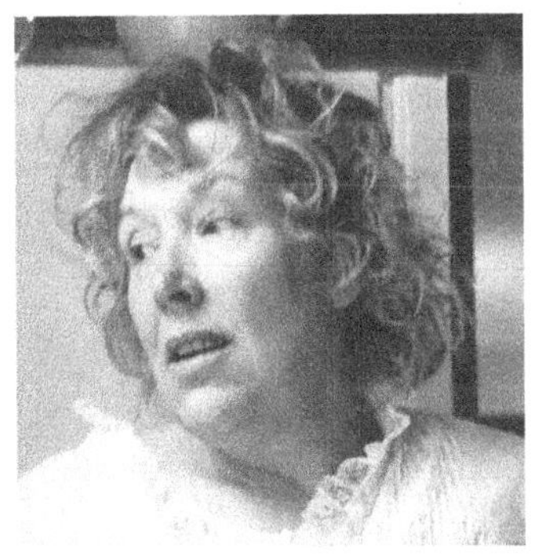

Pam Gems was born in 1925 in Mudeford, near Christchurch, in what was then Dorset, on the south coast of England. Her father, a Welsh ex-coalminer, died when she was six years old, leaving her mother to bring up Pam and her two brothers on her own.

For most of her childhood Pam's family lived in poverty, reliant on charity from the parish church and the Salvation Army. At eleven, she won a scholarship to grammar school, where she flourished, but left at fifteen to go to work.

World War Two broke out and, in 1943 (when she turned eighteen), she joined the Women's Royal Naval Service, and worked with British and Canadian bomber squadrons. She writes about this in FINCHIE's WAR.

After the war, she went to Manchester University, where she studied psychology and met her future husband, Keith.

Always stage-struck, Gems wrote her first play when she was eight, and was an enthusiastic participant in school plays. At university, she joined the dramatic society, wrote skits, produced and directed. After university, she worked in audience research at the BBC – which she loathed – and became part of the 'Ban the Bomb' London beatnik scene, which included Ted Hughes, the poet, Sean Kenny, the designer, and Robert Bolt, the playwright.

After marrying and having her first two children, she and her husband moved to Wandsworth in South London, where she wrote radio plays, beginning an extraordinarily prolific writing career that produced over seventy plays and adaptations. Pam Gems is, without doubt, Britain's greatest woman dramatist, with only Agatha Christie having had more West End productions.

Agatha Christie had ten plays presented in the West End, at a time when the economics of the West End plays weren't as prohibitive as they later became. Pam Gems had six, arguably seven, plays produced in the West End. The first was DUSA FISH STAS and VI, at the Mayfair, presented by Michael Codron, followed by PIAF, at the Piccadilly, presented by the RSC, which also later produced CAMILLE at the Comedy, and THE BLUE ANGEL at the Globe. LOVING WOMEN was presented at the Arts Theatre, and MARLENE had a successful run at the Lyric. STANLEY, which played to full houses at the Olivier Theatre, was offered a West-End transfer by three managements, but the company turned down these offers in favour of a transfer to the Circle in the Square, off-Broadway, in New York, where it ran for six months.

One thing that especially fascinates in the depth of Pam Gems' writing is the prophetic element. She perceived, well in advance, the dangers facing the pampered and decadent West, which we now see unfolding. As Victor Hugo said: 'Adversity makes men and prosperity makes monsters.' Her approach is always positive, however. Like the Beatles' song, all you need is love.

Love is all you need.

Jonathan Gems

ALSO BY THE SAME AUTHOR

Betty's Wonderful Christmas

Go West Young Woman

Queen Christina

Piaf

Camille

Pasionaria

Deborah's Daughter

Marlene

Stanley

The Snow Palace

King Ludwig of Bavaria

Mrs. Pat

Ethel

Not Joan the Musical

The Socialists

Dusa, Fish, Stas, and Vi

Aunt Mary

Garibaldi, Si!

The Incorruptible

The Treat

Franz Into April

Up in Sweden

Next Please

The Synonym

The Whippet

The Russian Princess

The Burning Man

A Builder by Trade

The Nourishing Lie

Mr Watts

In Donegal

Cluster

Down West

The Country House Sale

Ladybird, Ladybird

In The Hothouse

Guin for Guinevere

Marine

The Project

You Should Be Pleased He Likes Me

What Luck

An Ordinary Woman

We Never Do What They Want

Stella Campbell

Finchie's War

The Leg-Up

Maytime

Mabel's Bistro

A Kind of Ecstasy

At The Window

Who Is Sylvia?

ADAPTATIONS

Sarah B Divine!

My Name is Rosa Luxemburg

Rivers and Forests

Uncle Vanya

A Doll's House

The Seagull

Ghosts

Yerma

The Lady from the Sea

The Cherry Orchard

The Dance of Death

The Father

Hedda Gabbler

Three Sisters

The Little Mermaid

Behaving Badly

Stanley's Women

NOVELS

Mrs Frampton

Bon Voyage, Mrs Frampton

CONTENTS

PREFACE

Pam Gems was labelled a feminist writer (even a 'post-feminist' writer), but she was more than that. Feminism, for her, was just one aspect of a bigger picture: the dissolution and transmogrification of Western Society.

CAMILLE, THE BLUE ANGEL and THE ODD WOMEN were nineteenth century novels she adapted, in large part, because of their value in showing us the fixed society that had come before.

Pam was born in 1925, in a rural part of England that, in many respects, still resembled the Victorian age – with big houses inhabited by aristocrats and forelock-tugging servants, while the poor lived in hovels on the edge of starvation, dependent on alms from the Church.

As a young teenager, she worked in a factory straight out of Dickens's *Hard Times*. At eighteen, she joined the WRENS, and witnessed the radical changes brought about by WW2, which put the Attlee government in power – a revolutionary government intent upon putting an end to the class system.

The idiocies of the 'officer class,' had taught the people they were just as capable (if not more capable) than the mentally ill upper-crusters who had commanded them during the war.

At the same time, a loss of faith in the Church (not least because of its class arrogance) created a vacuum that filled with nihilism, hedonism, muddled dreams of a socialist utopia, and a new philosophy – Existentialism – which preached that meaning and purpose weren't conferred by Church or State but by each person individually.

In short, the fixed structure of society, painstakingly established over more than a thousand years, was shattered. The only constants remaining – apart from the basic instinct to survive – were Christmas, football, and the biological imperative to reproduce.

After the war, society atomized into nuclear families, each one a small boat on a vast ocean. Only the ultra-rich, at the top of society, retained the extended family and its cohesive customs and traditions. The rest of us were on our own.

And when the contraceptive pill was deployed in the 1960's, together with cures for syphilis and the media promotion of 'free love,' the nuclear family itself came under stress.

At the end of the '60's, the British divorce rate was 6%. By the end of the '70's, it was 52%, and single-parent families, once a rarity, were commonplace.

To compound this dissolution of structure, governments tore down what they called 'slum neighborhoods' (often well-built Victorian terraced cottages with gardens) replacing them with high-rise blocks, thus destroying local communities. Public services established by church-going Victorians and Edwardians, such as public swimming baths, public laundries, common land, cricket and football pitches, parks, public benches, and public toilets were sold off to property developers and banks. The police were taken off the beat, their mission changed to serving the state rather than the people in their local communities.

And, while this was happening, non-enforcement of the monopoly laws led to the decimation of small and medium-sized businesses, the destruction of our once-thriving high streets by chain-stores and supermarkets, and the devouring of family farms by large, élite-owned, agribusiness combines.

The dismantling of British society further accelerated with the removal of its borders and sovereignty when annexed by the European Union. New taxes were imposed, such as V.A.T., to feed the EU. Thousands of new regulations were imposed. Unelected assemblies were installed to manage Britain's EU-designated regions. Large, well-rooted communities in Wales, the Midlands, and the North were wiped out by the government complying with EU policies that demanded war on the coal-mining, ship-building, car, steel and fishing industries, resulting in the collapse of yet more indigenous communities.

To add to Britain's woes, the world's poor were encouraged to flood into the country, and the indignation this produced was nastily branded as 'racist' by state authorities and the complicit corporate media. The same corporate media that disparaged Britain's imperialist past, while it strenuously promoted the imperialism of the European Union.

The insecurity and anxiety produced by these all-out attacks on British society were treated with drugs from a ruthlessly profiteering chemical industry and, an expanding and invasive bureaucracy of apparatchiks and social workers.

Pam Gems perceived all this and offered insights, theories, and options. Although women were her primary concern, her philosophy equally embraced the challenges facing men.

In GARIBALDI, SI! she presents an idealized picture of a man in the fullness of his manhood. In UP IN SWEDEN, she portrays the terrifying void facing young men. She further delves into issues confronting men in LOVING WOMEN, FRANZ INTO APRIL, THE SOCIALISTS, and STANLEY.

Pam Gems made it her mission to write good parts for women and to support women playwrights and directors but, in the Ibsen tradition, her fundamental purpose was in diagnosing the realities, delusions, and maladies of our times.

Jonathan Gems

THE ODD WOMEN

a play for the screen by Pam Gems
adapted from the novel by George Gissing

THE ODD WOMEN

EXT. WELSH HILLS – DAY

There is no wind. The trees are in their full glory; the meadows and fields green and lush. No wind.

SUPERIMPOSE CAPTION: *The Welsh Hills 1872*

On a hillside, on a level site with shade from a fine oak, a PICNIC is taking place. The blue, yellow and pale pink of the girls' dresses shimmer in the light as they move about.

Preparing the picnic are VIRGNIA MADDEN – tall, golden-haired, soft-featured – and RHODA NUNN, a tall, dark, striking girl.

They assist the old NANNY, who spreads a brown tartan rug on the ground, and then the linen tablecloth over it. They set out the ample food, cutlery and napkins.

MONICA (Virginia's younger sister) helps a little, but strolls away, dreamy-faced, making a daisy-chain. The others smile, indulgent.

ALICE MADDEN, the eldest sister, who is short and less well-favoured, but pleasant in her pretty dress, brings the rest of the picnic from the gig – helped by the GROOM.

She inspects the efforts of the others with satisfaction.

> MONICA
>
> (*Calls*) Papa!

ROOKS fly up from the oak tree.

Their father, DR MADDEN, climbs the hill towards them, waving his wideawake hat. MONICA flies down the hill to meet him.

Followed by calls of 'Monica!' Monica!' from the others – DR MADDEN fondly catches MONICA by the waist, arresting her flight.

MONICA

Isn't it lovely? Make it go on forever.

He bows, accepting her command. She stands on a tuffet, and holds out her daisy-chain. He crowns her gravely.

MONICA

(*Ecstatic*) I am the Queen of the castle!

DR MADDEN

(*Laughing*) And I am the dirty rascal!

MONICA

No! You are Merlin!

She makes magic passes with her arms. He does likewise, then he hurries on ahead.

DR MADDEN

Come and see. Come and see!

MONICA

What? What?

EXT. WELSH HILLS – LATER

DR MADDEN is setting up his TRIPOD and CAMERA. The GIRLS and the GROOM scurry to and fro, assisting at his command. He is nervous of them damaging his photographic plates and camera, and fusses.

RHODA who, indicated by the doctor's polite smiles seems not to be a member of the family, is less perturbed. She watches the assembly of the equipment with a frowning interest, even shaking her head at the GROOM when he hands DR MADDEN the wrong piece, and picks out the right piece of the tripod to be assembled.

DR MADDEN squints at her, surprised.

DR MADDEN

Thank you, my dear.

The GROOM remains stolid and unimpressed at being shown up.

The GIRLS change places, composing themselves for the picture.

DR MADDEN messes about under the cloth, then emerges and comes forward to adjust the composition. Should they wear hats? He decides no, and returns to the camera.

ON: VIRGINIA, as a thought strikes her, and her face falls.

VIRGINIA

But Papa, you won't be in it!

ALICE

Oh, you must. (*To the others*) He must!

DR MADDEN stops in his tracks, and turns, thinking.

The others wait for him to find a solution.

RHODA

I'll take the photograph.

NANNY

Oh, Miss Rhoda!

DR MADDEN

I'm afraid it's much too complicated.

But RHODA walks firmly towards the camera. Her level expression changes his mind and, wanting to be in the picture, he shows her what to do. He begins to leave, then anxiously dodges back to make sure she understands.

Satisfied that she does, he hurriedly takes his place among the GIRLS in the centre of the picture.

RHODA, her head under the cloth, gets ready to take the picture.

RHODA

I'll take it on three. One ... Two ... Three!

She takes the picture.

FREEZE ON: the happy photo of the MADDEN FAMILY.

DISSOLVE TO:

INT. DRAPER'S SHOP – DAY

Ping! As a little wooden container, in an overhead trolley, sweeps across the width of the shop.

SUPERIMPOSE CAPTION: *Seven Years Later.*

The shop is sizable. In one corner, a GIRL is struggling to put rolls of cloth back on shelves after a sale.

There are long wooden counters; drawers with sample buttons and haberdashery tacked to the front; displays of lace collars, and trimmings for hats.

In another section, domestic uniforms are on display. There is a bridal area, and another section for widows' weeds.

The counters are manned by YOUNG MEN and YOUNG WOMEN ASSISTANTS.

An OLDER WOMAN assists a CUSTOMER who is trying on a hat.

The FLOOR-WALKER, an older man with a stiff face and rigid walk, moves about supervising. Only his eyes, with a hint of rage in them, have mobility.

He bears down on a YOUNG MAN who almost drops a mountain of parcels. His CUSTOMER is leaving without buying. Too late to intercept the Customer himself, the FLOORWALKER turns on the YOUNG MAN, who flinches with anxiety.

ON: the slender back of a GIRL, on a ladder, replacing heavy bales of cloth.

The FLOORWALKER grazes her with his eyes. The GIRL is struggling but he does nothing to help her. Then he notices, with disfavour, a bale of cloth still on the floor. He is about to approach her when the DOORBELL RINGS.

NEW ANGLE: A customer enters. It is RHODA – now thirty. She is tall and pale, with dark hair. Her movements are decisive, her clothes plain. Her shrewd eyes, and the firmness of her manner distract from the attractiveness of her full mouth and drooping eyelids. There is something about her that is subtle, unconventional, and challenging.

The GIRL, aware of someone behind her, leaps off the ladder – flustered and warm with the effort of replacing the bales. It is MONICA.

The shock is mutual. RHODA's mouth drops open in surprise. MONICA's face shows the pain of her humiliation. She wants to slip away, but it's not possible.

> RHODA
> Monica! What on earth are you doing here?

> MONICA
> (*Tries a cheery smile*) Attempting to earn a living it seems.

> RHODA
> But, my dear! How long have you … ?

> MONICA
> (*Moving away, whispers*) We're not allowed to have conversations.

RHODA

(*Following her, and lifting some cloth, as though deciding*) Your father ... ?

MONICA

He died.

RHODA

I'm so sorry. I didn't know. And Virginia? Alice?

RHODA looks about as if expecting to see them.

MONICA

They ... They're living in Clapham.

RHODA's eyes flick at the unfashionable address.

RHODA

I see. Do they, also ...

MONICA

(*Cutting a snip of cloth, as for a sample, low*) It's very difficult to find anything without training.

RHODA

How long have you been here?

RHODA glances at the other assistants, noting their difference in class.

MONICA

A year. (*With a flash of spirit.*) One of us must earn something!

RHODA

My dear, I'm so sorry. Do forgive me. Take my card. My friend and I have a typewriting school. You must have heard of them. The new business machines. We're finding posts for women all over London.

MONICA slips the card into her waist pocket, and puts the cloth samples in an envelope.

> MONICA
>
> Will that be all, Miss?

> RHODA
>
> Come and see us. Come tomorrow. You do have Sundays?

MONICA nods, escorting her to the door.

> RHODA
>
> (*At the door*) Do come. All of you. Please.

RHODA glances at TWO FEMALE ASSISTANTS who, profiting from the absence of the Floorwalker, are giggling noisily, as they tease a YOUNG MALE CO-WORKER.

RHODA gives MONICA a brilliant smile, and goes.

MONICA, shaken by the unexpected meeting, feels faint. Her colleague, young MR BULLIVANT, whose constant gazing at her betrays his attachment, sidles towards her.

> BULLIVANT
>
> (*Cockney*) Can I get you some water, Miss Madden?

She smiles and shakes her head.

> BULLIVANT
>
> (*Consulting his half-hunter pocket watch*) Nearly seven. Only another hour ...

THREE WOMEN sweep into the shop.

MONICA runs about, dancing attendance on them. She pulls out more and more lace for their inspection until the counter is foaming.

INT. DORMITORY – DAY

A long, bleak room with rows of beds on both sides. It is Sunday.

GIRLS are laughing and cheerful as they get ready to go out. They put on their best clothes, and noisy hats.

ON: MONICA, at the end of the dormitory, finishing her toilette with care. She has laid out her things on the bed. Stockings, gloves, hat. She picks them up as she needs them, in contrast to the raucous group at the other end, who leave a litter of discarded clothes, boots, and stockings behind them.

EXT. DORMITORY AND YARD – DAY

At the side exit, MONICA is jostled aside by GIRLS barging out into the yard.

MONICA'S POV: GIRL #1 is in the yard, laughing with THREE YOUNG MEN.

PAN TO: GIRL #2 teasing BULLIVANT flirtatiously. He turns his head, and gazes at Monica.

NEW ANGLE: MONICA sets off across the yard towards the gate.

BULLIVANT lifts his best hat as she passes him, but she merely smiles briefly, hardly noticing him.

EXT. CORNER OF THE STREET – DAY

The Dormitory Building is in the background.

MONICA arrives at the street corner, and is about to cross the road when the FLOORWALKER looms up behind her.

                    FLOORWALKER
          Going out, Miss Madden?

MONICA nods. He blocks her progress. Her eyes flicker rebelliously.

FLOORWALKER

That's it. Bodily recreation. Where are you off to?

MONICA

My sisters.

FLOORWALKER

Across the river, eh?

He considers the matter as though undecided whether to permit this particular excursion.

MONICA waits, her eyes down. He holds her for another sadistic moment then, with a dismissive nod ...

FLOORWALKER

Get on with you then.

She goes, conscious of his gaze on her back.

EXT. BY THE RIVER – DAY

Because of the fine weather, everyone is out. There are BOATS on the water: pleasure boats, rowing boats and skiffs.

MONICA walks by the river, deep in thought. Rhoda's visit is on her mind. She frowns to herself, then gazes reflectively across the water.

EXT. ANOTHER PART OF THE RIVER AND BRIDGE – DAY

A MAN is standing on the bridge. This is EDMUND WIDDOWSON. He is in his forties, saturnine, his eyes deep-set and almost invisible under his hat. From his clothes, he appears prosperous.

After a pause, he walks across the bridge and strolls along the riverside.

TWO GIRLS pass, and he slightly turns his head.

He sits down and watches PEOPLE go by. He turns his head again as a FINE-LOOKING WOMAN and her HUSBAND pass by. ANOTHER GIRL passes, alone.

He gets up and follows her. But, after a few moments, she increases her step, and runs to meet a YOUNG MAN.

WIDDOWSON walks on.

Then, ahead of him, he sees MONICA, pale and shining in her yellow dress, sitting on a seat, and gazing at the river. He's transfixed by her.

He walks past.

A little further on, he turns and retraces his steps.

He walks past her again, observing her more closely. She is, again, unaware of him.

He goes as far as the next bridge then, despite himself, retraces his steps. As he reaches her, he pauses for a second, and is about to address her.

She rises abruptly, having come to the decision to visit Rhoda.

She almost bumps into him.

He raises his hat.

WIDDOWSON

I beg your pardon.

MONICA

(*Automatically, without looking at him.*) I'm so sorry.

She walks quickly away.

He looks after her then, grasping his stick with sudden purpose, walks off in the same direction, passing a CHILD throwing a stick for a DOG.

MATCH CUT TO:

EXT. MARY'S HOUSE – GARDEN – DAY

A SPANIEL comes lolloping up to the TEA TABLE, in the garden of MARY's house in Chelsea.

Seated in basket chairs are: VIRGINIA, ALICE, MONICA and RHODA.

VIRGINIA, her golden hair fading, is now painfully thin. ALICE, now stocky, apologizes for her existence with every movement. Yet, what she says often betrays an inner indignation.

The sisters fall gratefully on the dog.

> VIRGINIA

Oh, you love!

> ALICE

What a dear boy. Here boy!

> VIRGINIA

Such a darling.

> ALICE

(*Looking round at the beautiful spring garden*) And the lilacs!

> VIRGINIA

We so miss it all.

> RHODA

Your father made no provision?

ALICE

He intended to insure his life. We spoke of it.

RHODA

And nothing from the sale of the house?

VIRGINIA

I'm afraid with the mortgage ...

MARY comes out of the house with a quick step.

She is in her thirties, fine-skinned, good-looking, with the easy, elegant clothes of a 'born lady.'

MONICA

My father had every intention of providing for us.

MARY

I'm so sorry! Do forgive me ...

RHODA

Alice, this is Mary. My old school-friend, Virginia. My friend and colleague, Mary Barfoot.

ALICE, trying to get out of her basket chair, gets stuck. She tips over and has to be rescued.

MARY

And you must be Monica. (*To RHODA*) Delightful. (*She gives Monica her hand.*) Rhoda's told me about you.

IDA, the maid, crosses the lawn with a heavily-laden tray.

MARY

Ah! (*With a smile*) Let's have some tea!

EXT. MARY'S HOUSE – GARDEN – DAY – LATER

ALICE and VIRGINIA are voraciously hungry, bending over their plates in glazed concentration.

RHODA, sharp-eyed, whispers an instruction to IDA, who looks surprised, then hurries back into the house.

MONICA, conscious of what is being betrayed, shakes her head firmly when offered more to eat.

MARY, reading Monica, turns from VIRGINIA.

> MARY
>
> (*To MONICA*) So, you've just had a birthday?

> ALICE
>
> (*Excited*) Yes!

> VIRGINIA
>
> Her twenty-first!

> ALICE
>
> Her twenty-first!

> MONICA
>
> (*Light*) Farewell youth.

> RHODA
>
> Oh, twenty-one, thirty-one, who cares? You're not aching for matrimony, I trust?

> ALICE
>
> (*Happily*) Oh, Monica's bound to marry, with her looks.

> VIRGINIA
>
> We're so hoping . . .

ALICE

Then we can keep house for her, and have a nice garden again.

MONICA

(*To RHODA, surprised*) You don't approve of marriage?

MARY throws her head back and chuckles.

MARY

Rhoda has other aims.

MONICA

Oh? What?

RHODA

To create a race of hard-hearted women for a start.

ALICE

Oh but . . .

VIRGINIA

(*Giggles*) Rhoda, you haven't changed a bit!

ALICE

But surely . . . Aren't women put on this earth . . . I mean, isn't the whole point of being a woman . . . ?

MONICA

Miss Nunn is joking.

IDA appears with a plate of delicious pink cold beef.

RHODA

Not at all. Have some beef. Do join me. I'm shockingly irregular. I had no lunch. I shall feel a fool eating alone.

She flashes her warm, brilliant smile disarmingly, and sets to like a hungry boy. So, VIRGINIA and ALICE are able to join in happily. MARY casts a bright eye on RHODA, approving of her kind gesture, and its skillful execution.

EXT. ANOTHER PART OF MARY'S GARDEN – DAY

MARY, RHODA, and MONICA stroll among the lilacs and beds of wallflowers.

Behind them, VIRGINIA and ALICE continue to tuck in.

RHODA

You mean, you work six full days a week?

They move off through the dark laurel shrubbery.

MARY

No early closing?

CUT TO:

At the table, IDA smiles and sets down a large plate of cakes. Then refills VIRGINIA and ALICE's teacups.

CUT TO:

WIDESHOT of the shrubbery.

We see MARY, RHODA and MONICA briefly, as they pass a clearing.

RHODA

I should like to set fire to it!

MONICA

I don't think you would, Miss Nunn.

They disappear behind the bushes.

MARY

(*Off screen*) You mean just board and keep? No salary?

RHODA

(*OS*) Five children? And cooking?

MARY

(*OS*) Your poor sister!

RHODA

(*OS*) But you say she gave it up?

The three women reappear, coming back along the gravel path.

MONICA

They dismissed her. She was ill.

RHODA

(*Abrupt*) Come along.

NEW ANGLE: MONICA follows RHODA and MARY across the grass towards a LARGE WHITE CONSERVATORY.

MARY looks over at the sisters, eating at the table, and decides to join them.

RHODA and MONICA enter the conservatory.

INT. CONSERVATORY – DAY

RHODA takes the lid off a large black typewriter on a marble-topped table, covered with papers.

RHODA

There! What do you make of that?

MONICA looks at the machine without enthusiasm.

MONICA

It looks dreadfully complicated.

RHODA

Oh, you mustn't be faint-hearted. Come, I'll show you.

RHODA sits at the table and rolls up her sleeves. She inserts the paper and begins to type. MONICA watches, fascinated, despite herself.

RHODA

(*Pulls out the sheet.*) There you are.

MONICA

(*Reads*) 'I am your humble and obedient servant. My keys are the keys to freedom.'

RHODA indicates for MONICA to sit and try the machine.

MONICA

Oh, but I couldn't!

RHODA

(*A flicker of tigerish rage*) Of course you can.

MONICA sits.

RHODA

This is the carriage release. You see? Now, insert the paper. That's right. Straighten it up. Good. Now push the lever back. These are the margin releases. I won't bother you with those just now. Have a try.

MONICA looks doubtful.

RHODA

Just press the keys. Use your forefingers. Like this.

She demonstrates.

MONICA types her name. It comes out as: mobica maddwn.

RHODA

Good. Of course, with training, you'll be able to use all your fingers and work at speed. That commands

a higher salary. May I ask how much they pay you at
the shop?

MONICA

(*Unwillingly*) Seven and six a week.

RHODA

(*Shocked*) The three of you? On seven and six a
week? It's impossible!

MONICA

I do receive board and lodging.

RHODA waves her hand dismissively.

RHODA

You must come to us at once. Tomorrow. You can
share Millie's flat. Are you good at figures?

MONICA

(*With an alarmed shake of the head*) No.

She moves away.

RHODA

(*Surprised*) The idea doesn't appeal to you?

MONICA

We should have nothing to live on.

RHODA

We advance a salary during training. You can repay
us at a later date. I can assure you, you'll be far better
off.

MONICA

I'm sorry. You're being very kind. It's just that ... I'm
afraid I'm not the least bit clever, and I can't afford
to ... to take risks.

RHODA

My dear, I understand, believe me. I want to help.

MONICA

(*Looks round at the glorious room*) But why us? Why
me?

RHODA

We're old friends.

MONICA looks warily at the typewriter.

RHODA

Office work is not the most exciting prospect, but it's a
step. For all of us. Don't you see? There are solutions.
That we ourselves can create. And why shouldn't we
be part of the business world? Know what's going on,
instead of being dependent?

MONICA smiles politely, moves to the window, and looks out.

RHODA

I promise you, you will be so much better placed.

RHODA joins MONICA at the window.

THEIR POV: VIRGINIA and ALICE are talking to MARY on the
lawn, and petting the DOG.

MONICA

I expect you see a change in them.

RHODA

Yes.

MONICA

They miss the country.

RHODA

Think about it. Please. Will you?

MONICA

It's very kind of you to offer, but . . .

RHODA

Don't decide now. (*She looks at her with a glowing, thrilling gaze, willing her to agree.*) You're just the sort of girl we need. You'll do splendidly, take my word for it. Come and try.

EXT. TUBE STATION – DAY

MONICA comes out of the tube station – a press of PEOPLE behind her. She walks quickly along the road towards us, swinging her sunshade, her mood elevated.

NEW ANGLE: WIDDOWSON comes out of the tube station. He sees her in the distance and follows.

EXT. STREET NEAR THE DRAPER'S – DAY

As MONICA approaches the Draper's Shop, she hears a step behind her and glances around briefly. Seeing nothing, she crosses the road.

Unseen by her, WIDDOWSON has passed her. Now, he crosses the road too.

EXT. DELIVERY YARD ENTRANCE – DAY

ON: MONICA at the entrance to the Draper's Delivery Yard. She finds her latchkey and opens the small door in the large door into the yard.

She crosses the yard and lets herself into the back of the shop.

Outside the entrance, WIDDOWSON looks up at the fascia of the establishment.

FADE OUT.

INT. DORMITORY – NIGHT

The GIRLS are getting ready for bed.

GIRL #1 goes from one person to another with a blue paper CONE OF SWEETS, and is thanked profusely.

She reaches MONICA at the end of the room; makes to turn away; but changes her mind.

> GIRL #1
>
> 'Ere, want one?

> MONICA
>
> Thank you.

> GIRL #2
>
> Wonder 'ow she got those, ay?

> GIRL #3
>
> Don' arsk questions.

They all laugh.

GIRL #2 hops into bed, fully-dressed.

> GIRL #1
>
> Ain'tcha gonna take yer clothes off?

> GIRL #2
>
> I might when me feet warm up. 'Ere, you'll never
> guess where me an' Nell went today.

THREE GIRLS, whispering and giggling, sit on GIRL #2's bed.

At the window, GIRL #4 brushes her hair and listens.

> GIRL #4
>
> I don't believe it.

> GIRL #2
>
> Why not?

GIRL #4

'Cause you don't meet nothin' worth a tanner in a
public bar, that's why.

GIRL #1

You can!

GIRL #4

My word, you don't. You wanna take a tip from the
duchess.

MONICA

Me? What about?

GIRL #4

(*Genial*) Come on, Miss Innocent. We seen you!

MONICA

What do you mean?

GIRL #4

What's more ... (*She peeks through the curtains.*) 'E's
still there.

GIRL #3 is lighting the old candles in the CANDLESTICKS, and
placing one by each bed. GIRL #1 cranes out the window.

GIRL #1

You're a dark horse, Madden.

MONICA

What do you mean?

MONICA, her hair down, looks out of the window.

HER POV: The Street. A LAMPLIGHTER is lighting a lamp and
WIDDOWSON moves away. But not before MONICA has noticed his
hat, coat, and silver-topped cane.

She stretches for a further look.

MONICA

You mean the old man in the street?

GIRL #4

Never mind his age. Better than the four-ale bar, ay
Rose?

GIRL #3 (ROSE) smiles, and looks out the window.

GIRL #4

You ought to tell 'im, Madden.

ROSE hops across the floor in her bare feet, and jumps into bed. The
other GIRLS get into bed severally, except GIRL #4, who lingers by
the window, finishing her hair.

MONICA gets into bed.

GIRL #4

Tell 'im to drop you at the end of the road. You'll get
us all in trouble.

MONICA

(*Muffled by her bedclothes*) I don't know him.

ON GIRL #4 looking out of the window.

HER POV: The Lamplighter has gone. But WIDDOWSON is standing
under the lighted lamp.

CLOSE ON: WIDDOWSON looking up at the dormitory window. HIS
POV: GIRL #4 drawing the curtain.

GIRL #4 draws the curtain and gets into her bed.

GIRL# 2

Whitsun next week. We shan't need candles.

GIRL #4

They keep you warm.

ROSE

(*Sighs*) What I couldn't do to a mutton pie.

MONICA lies, eyes wide open, thinking about Rhoda's offer.

GIRL #1

(*Sleepy*) Come on, Madden. What's 'is name?

MONICA

(*Vexed*) I've told you. I don't know him.

INT. DRAPER'S SHOP – DAY

The shop is busy.

WIDDOWSON is standing in front of her at the counter.

MONICA is shocked. But his manner is polite and composed.

He bows slightly.

MONICA

May I help you?

WIDDOWSON

I ... I ... I should like ... (*He cannot take her eyes off
her.*) Perhaps you would be kind enough to ...

He breaks away, and notices a DISPLAY OF GLOVES.

WIDDOWSON

Gloves?

MONICA

Certainly, sir. Fabric or skin?

WIDDOWSON

Oh, leather.

MONICA smiles politely and moves along the counter. He never
takes his eyes off her.

MONICA

Have you a preference to colour?

WIDDOWSON

What colour would you suggest?

MONICA

Grey is very fashionable just now.

WIDDOWSON

Do you like grey?

MONICA smiles without reply, and turns away. He watches her back and her profile as she looks among the stock.

She shows him the gloves. He looks over the first tray. She lifts down another tray. And another.

The FLOORWALKER approaches. But WIDDOWSON shoots him a dismissive glance and he moves away.

WIDDOWSON

Which do you suggest?

MONICA

How much did you wish to spend?

WIDDOWSON

It's of no consequence. (*He picks out a pair of gloves.*)
Perhaps you'd be kind enough to try these on, for size.

She nods, pulls and fits the kid gloves he has picked out. She looks at her hand in the elegant gloves. He watches her expression.

WIDDOWSON

I'll take them.

She takes off the gloves, pulling at them gently.

WIDDOWSON

I should be obliged if you would make a little parcel
for me.

MONICA

As a gift?

He nods, and watches her as she finds ribbon and paper, and
skillfully makes the little package.

The FLOORWALKER watches as WIDDOWSON leaves with his
package. He beckons MONICA to a discreet corner.

FLOORWALKER

Perhaps, Miss Madden, you would be good enough to
explain your conduct.

MONICA

I beg your pardon?

FLOORWALKER

Twenty minutes to sell a pair of gloves? You know the
rule. No followers.

MONICA

He was a customer!

FLOORWALKER

Don't lie to me girl. I've had information. Don't think
we're fooled by all this superior manner. I've dealt
with your sort before. It won't be the first time a girl
has been dismissed.

MONICA

Dismissed? There's no question of that.

She walks away, leaving him dumbfounded. He recovers himself
and follows her. She turns on him.

MONICA

(*Quietly*) I am leaving this establishment.

MR BULLIVANT, nearby, comes forward, his face expressing dismay. The OTHER GIRLS approach, listening, agog at the drama.

FLOORWALKER

(*Blocking her path*) Just a minute ...

MONICA

(*Side-stepping him*) Please be good enough to accept
my notice to quit. As of this instance.

She dives quickly, retrieves her shawl from behind the counter, and whirls past him.

Outraged, he follows her.

FLOORWALKER

Found a better billet, Miss? Ay? Ay?

MONICA exits swiftly through the front door.

The FLOORWALKER rounds on the staff who have crowded forward, their faces alive with excitement.

FLOORWALKER

What's going on? Get back.

They scurry in all directions.

FLOORWALKER

There'll be a few more dismissals for misconduct
before the morning's out.

But the staff are not fooled. As he goes into his office, and slams the door, they smile.

EXT. TYPING SCHOOL AND STREET – DAY

A pale, two storey Victorian school building with lots of windows.

SOUND of forty typewriters clacking.

INT. MAIN ROOM – TYPING SCHOOL – DAY

FORTY GIRLS are seated at small tables, typing. The NOISE is deafening.

ON: MONICA typing with difficulty. She pauses, and grimaces.

MILLIE, a pleasant, plain girl, who is supervising, is at her side at once. She bends over MONICA, demonstrating.

She take's Monica's place and demonstrates the finger movements.

MONICA nods.

MILLIE rattles off a quick line of type. MONICA pulls a hopeless face. They both laugh.

MILLIE gets up and moves off to another pupil. MONICA tries again.

But her eyes stray to the window.

HER POV: TWO PRETTILY DRESSED YOUNG WOMEN in fine bonnets, pass by.

This depresses her. But she smiles up at MILLIE as she passes down the aisle once more. And begins to type again.

INT. OFFICE – TYPING SCHOOL – DAY

Behind the netted window between the office and the schoolroom, MARY and RHODA pause briefly, watching their new pupil.

RHODA returns to her desk.

MARY

She's much too pretty of course.

RHODA

(*Off screen*) We can't be seen as a refuge for the ugly.

MARY turns, surprised. RHODA looks up from her desk, coolly.

RHODA

Oh, they'd like that.

She bends to her own work. MARY returns to her desk.

MARY

Yes. Any excuse to dismiss our efforts.

RHODA

There's something about her. She's not aware of
herself yet, of course, but there's something there.

MARY looks at her, then fishes in her desk for a letter. She pauses
for a second, then throws the letter across to Rhoda.

MARY

It's from Bella ... Royston.

RHODA lifts her eyebrows, picks up the letter, reads it, and throws
it down.

MARY

What do you think?

RHODA

Oh, a small cheque, if you must. (*She catches MARY's
eye*) You're not suggesting that we have her back
here?

MARY looks at her appealingly. RHODA gets up, irritable, and
turns on her.

RHODA

She knew the man had a wife!

MARY

Yes, yes.

RHODA

We are not a social dustbin. We need women of ... of a special ...

MARY

I know. She <u>is</u> intelligent. One of our most ...

RHODA

I suppose she rushed off, thinking herself some idiot heroine ...

MARY

She <u>was</u> in love ...

RHODA

Oh yes. All this bliss we're promised.

MARY

You've never ... ?

RHODA

No. And no wish to.

MARY

(*Slight pause.*) We can at least be kind.

RHODA

(*Ferocious*) No! That is just what we cannot be! We cannot allow ourselves to be soft. Weak. If we are to ...

MARY

You can't change human nature.

RHODA

Why not? We … (*She bangs herself on the chest*) We
are the world. And I, for one, intend to change it.

MARY takes the letter and puts it back in her desk.

MARY

There are worse things than being in love.

RHODA looks at her, thoughtfully.

EXT. RIVERSIDE – DAY

MONICA and MILLIE are strolling happily by the river.

MILLIE stops short.

MILLIE

Oh! I almost forgot! Do you mind if we call at Miss
Barfoot's? There's an article for the publisher.

MONICA

You go. They'll be glad of a rest from me. I'm doing so
stupidly!

MILLIE

Nonsense. Do come.

MONICA

I think I'll avoid Miss Nunn's gimlet eye.

They laugh.

MILLIE

Rightyo. Last one in makes the toast!

MILLIE marches off with a cheerful wave.

MONICA strolls by the river. She glances at the BOATS and,
returning her glance to the path, sees WIDDOWSON coming
straight for her.

Out of face, she looks away. He arrives and raises his hat. She nods distantly, and walks on, away from the river, and through the trees.

Just when she thinks she has lost him, he appears on the path in front of her.

> WIDDOWSON

I beg your pardon.

> MONICA

Not at all.

She tries to pass.

> WIDDOWSON

(*Shaking with tension*) I was hoping I might see you.

> MONICA

What for?

> WIDDOWSON

You were so courteous in the shop. I wanted to thank you for your kind assistance.

> MONICA

(*Looks at him coldly*) That is what I am paid for.

She walks on. He catches her up.

> WIDDOWSON

(*Clears his throat.*) Are you happy with your new occupation?

She quickens her step, puzzled at his knowing this.

> WIDDOWSON

They were not fit companions for you – the girls there.

> MONICA

Oh?

WIDDOWSON

Much too noisy.

MONICA

They deserve a little enjoyment.

WIDDOWSON

But they are not your sort.

MONICA

You know nothing about me.

WIDDOWSON

I know that you are now much better placed, Miss
Madden.

She hurries on, then turns on him

MONICA

How do you know my name?

WIDDOWSON

Miss Monica Madden. You are sharing a flat
near Regent's Park with Miss Mildred Vesper.
Thirty- two …

MONICA

Have you been following me?

He gazes at her humbly.

MONICA

How ridiculous!

She walks off and sits on a park bench overlooking the river.

WIDDOWSON

Please – allow me to give you my card.

She ignores him.

WIDDOWSON

I am most anxious that you don't misunderstand me.
All I ask is to make your acquaintance.

MONICA makes to rise.

WIDDOWSON

Please! I've been coming here every day since I first
saw you three weeks ago.

MONICA looks at him, disturbed by this declaration. He joins her on
the bench. A long pause. They both stare at the river. BOATS pass.
A ROWING-EIGHT passes.

WIDDOWSON

My word. That must take some energy.

MONICA

(*Stiffly*) I wonder their hands aren't raw.

WIDDOWSON

Do please … (*He offers his card again*)

MONICA

(*Shakes her head.*) I'm sorry. I'm afraid I don't know
you.

WIDDOWSON

May I not introduce myself? It's unconventional, I
agree …

MONICA

I'm sorry.

WIDDOWSON

Why?

MONICA

We have no mutual acquaintance.

WIDDOWSON

Surely that could be remedied? I should be delighted
for you to meet my sister-in-law. Or, if you would be
kind enough to introduce me to your family, your
friends ...

MONICA

How could I? There's no possible way. I don't know
you, Mr ...

WIDDOWSON

(*Eagerly.*) Widdowson. Edmund Widdowson.

MONICA

You must know that I couldn't introduce you to my
family. I should be hopelessly compromised. (*She
sighs.*) I wonder sometimes how people <u>do</u> meet.

WIDDOWSON

You are quite right. Thank you for making it clear.
The last thing I want is to cause you embarrassment.

He looks up at the bank behind, and the road beyond, where there's
a FINE CARRIAGE. The HORSE is restless.

WIDDOWSON

Ah, my animal is restless.

She follows his gaze – and is impressed by the carriage.

WIDDOWSON gives her his hand. She takes it, wanting to see the
horse.

They climb the bank to the road.

CUT TO:

ON: MONICA petting the horse, rubbing its nose.

WIDDOWSON brings something out of the carriage. It is the PACKET OF GLOVES. He presents it to her.

She shakes her head.

                    WIDDOWSON
     No. Please . . . I bought them for you. May we not
     disregard convention?

But she moves off.

                    WIDDOWSON
     (*Following*) Can I hope to see you next Sunday? I
     shall be here. And the Sunday after. And the one after
     that.

                    MONICA
     (*Impish, and emboldened now she's going*) How very
     boring for you.

                    WIDDOWSON
     No. Never.

He looks down at her, his eyes intense. Then he raises his hat formally, gets into the driving seat of the carriage, and trots off.

MONICA turns and realizes she still has the gloves. She walks down the bank, and opens the packet.

The GLOVES are beautiful. She strokes them, turning them over in the sun. And plays with the pearl buttons.

INT. MARY'S DRESSING ROOM AND STAIRS – NIGHT

MARY takes a last speculative look at herself in her dressing room mirror. She is wearing an evening dress of a gauzy material, with shimmering brilliants in her hair. She looks dazzling.

Satisfied, she leaves the room, crosses the landing, and descends the staircase.

Below her is EVERARD, a handsome man – tall, with an easy insolence – who looks up as IDA, the maid, takes his coat.

MARY

Ah, there you are!

INT. DRAWING ROOM AND HALL – NIGHT

EVERARD has been given a drink. He prowls, watched by MARY.

EVERARD

The house is looking well.

MARY

Having started on the abominable plumbing, it was hard to stop.

EVERARD

You've made splendid improvements.

MARY

I'm still dazed. And very grateful to your father.

EVERARD

Oh, the old man knew what he was doing. Matter of fact, I think he hoped we'd make a match of it. (*Light*) So much for parental aspirations. (*Slight pause.*) How are the good works?

MARY

I've taken a partner. You'll meet her. If she deigns to appear that is.

He raises his eyebrows. IDA, the maid appears at the door.

MARY

Ah!

IDA precedes MARY and EVERARD across the hall towards the Dining Room.

EVERARD

You're looking beautiful.

MARY

Rats. I've hardly had time to change.

EVERARD

Then you must have a secret.

MARY

No. No attachments.

She turns, smiling, but EVERARD's attention has been diverted by RHODA, who is coming down the stairs.

She is wearing a plain black dress and has dragged her hair back into a severe bun. Even so, something happens. He gazes up at her, and she down at him, for a second. Both are transfixed.

MARY

(*OS*) Rhoda, this is my cousin Everard. My friend, Rhoda Nunn.

INT. DINING ROOM – NIGHT

At dinner. A fire is roaring in the fireplace. IDA comes and goes quietly.

MARY

More lamb? (*She serves EVERARD generously*) And how is Tom?

EVERARD

As usual, iller than he says. (*Shrugs*) Anything rather than alarm Lil.

MARY

I must go down and see him. And Brian starving in
Cairo rather than – what was it? Live with a woman
who talks about what?

EVERARD

Plates in the main. Cutlery occasionally – but not with
the same passion.

RHODA gives him a cold look.

EVERARD

But I'm boring Miss Nunn. (*To RHODA*) Do you travel?
Have you been abroad?

RHODA

Never.

EVERARD

I almost envy you.

RHODA

(*Awkward*) Oh?

EVERARD

You have it all before you. The Bosphorous … The
first sunlight on the Sphinx … Tuscany in the
spring …

Despite herself, she is caught. He gazes at her.

INT. DINING ROOM – NIGHT – LATER

EVERARD

Not at all. Deserts can be devilish. Cold at night. This
is, of course, useful. When it was possible, we covered
ground in the dark. But you need decent roads.

RHODA

Extraordinary to find Roman beads, lying in the
desert.

MARY

(*Feeling a little left out*) How's Wilfred?

EVERARD

Alas, a changed man.

MARY

Oh? Why?

EVERARD

Married the most humourless woman in London.
Apparently, explaining his jokes is driving him out of
his mind.

MARY

Perhaps she has heard them before?

EVERARD

I swear not. He's a most inventive fellow.

RHODA

(*Shrugs*) Why will men marry fools?

EVERARD

A man has to marry someone.

RHODA

Why?

Their eyes connect. He smiles. She returns a level gaze.

INT. DRAWING ROOM – NIGHT

RHODA, slightly apart from the others, smokes a long, thin cigar.

> EVERARD
>
> So, having worked like the devil for the past ten
> years, I intend to do nothing. I shall see my beloved
> brother. Try and kick some sense into him. Persuade
> him to a warmer climate … and then enjoy myself.

> MARY
>
> You can't mean to do nothing at all.

> RHODA
>
> (*Languid*) Why not?

MARY looks at her in surprise. RHODA puts her feet up on the sofa, which EVERARD notices.

> RHODA
>
> What is your profession?

> EVERARD
>
> I'm an engineer.

She lifts her eyebrows.

> EVERARD
>
> There's still a lot of the world to be seen.

> MARY
>
> An infinite picture gallery is not my idea of
> enjoyment. What about … (*Chuckles*) … Satan and
> idle hands?

> EVERARD
>
> The busy make far more mischief, surely? Don't you
> think? Or does that conflict with your theories?

MARY

Yours seem convenient enough.

EVERARD

I have none. Except to enjoy myself.

MARY

No matter at whose expense!

EVERARD

I've never wished to behave badly. I'm much too
tender to hurt anyone. Surely, you know that?

An awkward silence. RHODA gets up abruptly and goes.

EVERARD

Oh dear. Have I chased her away?

MARY

Rhoda does as she pleases. She happens to be an
extraordinarily interesting woman.

EVERARD

I'm sure of it. I am on your side, you know. (*He rises to
his feet.*) I admire what you're trying to do.

MARY rings for IDA.

MARY

Nonsense. You despise women.

She goes out into the hall. EVERARD follows.

INT. HALL – NIGHT

EVERARD

(*Following her*) Damn. There goes my chance of
another sublime dinner.

IDA gives him his hat and coat.

EVERARD

Thank you, Ida.

IDA smiles at him fondly, and goes.

MARY

(*Opening the front door*) You idiot. Of course you must
come again. This house is as much yours as it is mine.

EVERARD

Good. (*Looking down at her*) When would you like
me?

MARY

(*Breaking away slightly*) Oh, you'll do as you want, as
always.

He bends, as though to kiss her, then plants a little kiss on her
cheek, and leaves.

INT. DRAWING ROOM – NIGHT

MARY enters the drawing room, and tends to the fire.

RHODA

(*Off screen*) He wasn't what I expected.

MARY jumps slightly at RHODA's voice. RHODA comes in and helps
herself to a nightcap.

MARY

Oh, Everard's full of charm.

MARY tidies her hair, looking in the glass. RHODA throws herself
on the sofa.

RHODA

Why did his father disinherit him?

MARY glances at her in the mirror, but makes no response, and moves away from the fireplace.

RHODA

He doesn't seem to resent that you benefited by it.

MARY

Oh, Everard would never hold a grudge.

RHODA is surprised by the warmth of her defence.

MARY

Still . . . we've the advantage of him.

RHODA

(*Curious*) How do you mean?

MARY

What can men do? It's over for them. They've made machines we can mind as well as they can. We're no longer at a disadvantage. What is more, my dear, we are involved in the most vital movement of our times. What can a man do?

RHODA

Free the working classes?

MARY laughs.

RHODA

Perhaps we should take him in hand?

MARY

Everard?

RHODA

(*Casual*) Why not?

MARY

If you take my advice, you will leave that particular
man well alone.

RHODA

Why? He seems harmless enough.

MARY

On the contrary. I happen to know he is a vicious
coward. And no friend to women.

RHODA is taken aback by the venom in MARY's tone.

EXT. RIVERSIDE – DAY

EDMUND WIDDOWSON, in a new frock coat, waits by the river. He
holds a small posy of flowers. He walks up and down, but there is
no sign of MONICA.

CUT TO:

EXT. RIVERSIDE – DAY – LATER

It is raining. PEOPLE run for shelter.

WIDDOWSON is still waiting, and getting soaked.

CUT TO:

EXT. RIVERSIDE – DAY – LATER

WIDDOWSON stands under a tree, sheltering from the rain.

WIDDOWSON

(*Voice-over*) My dear Miss Madden, I was so very
disappointed again this week not to see you. I daresay
you thought the weather uncertain and, indeed,
it has been raining. And I would, on no account,
have you incommoded. How the starlings chattered
afterwards. I must see you. Edmund Widdowson.

INT. TYPING SCHOOL – DAY

MONTAGE of MONICA at the typing school: arriving at the school; laughing with the other girls as they take off their coats; practicing typing with intent concentration; sitting with RHODA, who is teaching her book-keeping; back again at her typing desk; she is getting faster. MONICA and the other GIRLS putting on their coats and hats and leaving to go home. MONICA typing assiduously, with a small bunch of roses on her desk.

> WIDDOWSON
>
> (*V/O over montage*) I know that your work must take
> a great deal of your attention. I should so much like
> to hear of your progress. My garden is glorious with
> roses just now . . . (*Crossfade*) Thank you for your
> note. Naturally I am disappointed that you do not feel
> able to meet me. My sister-in- law has at-homes on
> Thursday evenings. I wonder if . . .

EXT. GROCERY SHOP AND STREET – DAY

MONICA and MILLIE leave the shop with food for their supper. They walk together, happily chatting.

Across the road, WIDDOWSON watches them.

INT. MONICA'S BEDROOM – NIGHT

MONICA is in bed, reading a letter.

> WIDDOWSON (V/O)
>
> . . . all I ask is to be allowed to see you. To pay court
> to you as any honest man. There is no question of my
> putting pressure on you. That is the last thing that
> I want. I cannot take your letter as a dismissal. You
> know my feelings for you, and I beg of you to think of
> me kindly. You have no idea of my present state . . .

MONICA turn over and bends down, finding a BOX under her bed. She carefully put the letter with the others.

Then she sits up in bed, thinking. Despite herself, the reality of a man so in love with her makes her feel triumphant.

INT. STAIRS AND BEDSIT – APARTMENT BUILDING – DAY

MARY climbs the stairs of a poor and dingy apartment building to the top floor, followed by a POLICEMAN.

POLICEMAN #2 waits for them at the top landing. When they reach him, he opens the door into a miserable room, and indicates the bed where a GIRL is lying.

She is dead.

MARY, very shocked, goes to the window, trying to compose herself.

POLICEMAN #1 approaches MARY. Sensing him, she turns and forces herself to cross the room and look down at the dead girl.

The beautiful, marble face looks serene and pensive.

MARY's eyes fill with tears. She grimaces with momentary rage, then compresses her lips and turns to POLICEMAN #1 and nods.

EXT. CHELSEA GARDENS – DAY

EVERARD walks briskly through Chelsea Gardens, veering as he sees RHODA, stiff and upright, sitting on a bench.

                              EVERARD
    Mary's not well … ?

                              RHODA
    So I believe.

She rises, drawing on her gloves, and walks off.

EVERARD

(*Beside her*) The inquest, no doubt. I see that you, too,
are ...

RHODA

Not in the least.

EVERARD

Oh come ...

RHODA

(*Stopping, black-faced*) Are you accusing me of
falsehood?

EVERARD

(*Matching her stride as she marches off.*) You prefer
not to give way to feeling?

RHODA

If I had any in the matter, I should certainly not feel
obliged to fulfill your notions of female sensibility.

EVERARD takes her hand, forcing her to halt.

EVERARD

Forgive me. I've upset you.

RHODA pulls her hand away irritably.

EVERARD

What's the matter?

The harshness of his voice affects her. She flicks him a quick look.
A GROUP OF PEOPLE pass by.

RHODA

(*Stiffly*) Mary wanted the wretched girl back. I didn't.
Now I'm to blame for her death.

She walks on. He catches her up. They continue together. He enjoys the view of her fine profile.

> EVERARD

Come.

His placating tone infuriates her. She quickens her step.

> EVERARD

I'll persuade her.

She gives a sneering little laugh, but her step slackens.

> EVERARD

I've no doubt you have the right of it.

> RHODA

Pray don't think I'm obliged for your good opinion.

They reach a corner, under the deep shade of a tree.

> EVERARD

She's bound to blame you. I believe she was fond of the girl. (*He tries to make her look at him, but she won't do it.*) Perhaps you should make allowances for human weakness.

She looks at him with a bright, malevolent stare.

> RHODA

Why?

He is half-repelled, half-attracted by her hardness.

> EVERARD

I admire your consistency.

He takes her hand to kiss it. She snatches it away.

            RHODA

That's enough! I suggest that you practice your
powers of irony elsewhere.

She walks off swiftly, her back straight, her skirt moving violently.

He raises his hat automatically and stands on his cane, watching
her. From his expression, the encounter seems to have put him in
a good mood.

EXT. RIVERSIDE – DAY

MONICA and WIDDOWSON are in a ROWING BOAT on the river.

The weather is idyllic, and she looks dazzlingly beautiful. He has
taken his hat off and looks younger and, because he is happy,
better-looking. MONICA gazes about her indolently, enjoying the
release from work. He never takes his eyes from her face.

They almost collide with ANOTHER BOAT.

MONICA laughs.

INT. OFFICE – TYPING SCHOOL – DAY

MARY is at her desk. She looks up and down again as RHODA
enters. It's obvious they aren't speaking.

RHODA takes her hat from the peg.

            RHODA

I've decided to leave.

            MARY

(*Her voice thick, head bent*) Whatever you wish.

            RHODA

Since we're no longer friends.

            MARY

Not on my side.

RHODA

I will not have you blame me.

MARY

I was upset!

MARY gets up and walks about, agitated.

MARY

Of course I don't blame you. The idea is ... surely a
little ... I mean, just a little sympathy.

RHODA

Why, when I feel none?

MARY looks at RHODA's composed face, and shakes her head at
RHODA's hardness.

MARY

Perhaps you're right to think of leaving.

Now RHODA is upset. She expects to be persuaded to stay. There is
an inner collapse. She is wounded. She lifts her chin with the hurt.

MARY

You may be wrong for this work.

RHODA's mouth drops open with shock.

MARY

Do you know what you're doing when you ask them
to give up marriage? It seems no sacrifice for you. I
don't know whether to feel envy or sorrow.

This pierces RHODA's armour.

MARY

(Seeing this, her voice softens) How can you judge
passion when you've never experienced it?

                    RHODA

I'm to behave like Bella Royston?

MARY's face hardens at this smack at a girl who is dead. But she tries again.

                    MARY

If you'd been there, I believe even your feelings …

                    RHODA

Oh, feelings.

She turns from the window, her eyes blazing.

                    RHODA

Do you think the great movements of civilisation are directed by feelings?

                    MARY

Yes.

MARY picks up papers from her desk with slightly trembling hands, skirts past RHODA, and leaves the room without another word.

A pause.

RHODA hears the outer door slam. She goes to the door of the office, and looks out at the empty silent schoolroom.

INT. TATE GALLERY – DAY

There's an animated buzz as PEOPLE marvel at the Pre-Raphaelite pictures.

MONICA and MILLIE, sharing and consulting a programme, move from painting to painting with fervent attention.

MONICA is stopped by the sight of WIDDOWSON at a distance. He bows, but does not approach.

MILLIE, turning back to MONICA, follows her gaze and sees WIDDOWSON.

> MILLIE

(*Whispers*) Is that him?

MONICA nods coolly, and walks on, and regards another painting. MILLIE can't resist taking another look.

She rejoins MONICA and whispers an enquiry. MONICA glances at WIDDOWSON briefly and nods.

> MILLIE

But he's old!

CUT TO:

Later.

MONICA and MILLE, sit on a central banquette, side by side, and fatigued.

WIDDOWSON can be seen from time to time, at a distance.

> MILLIE

Will you marry him?

> MONICA

No, of course not.

> MILLIE

I think you must be very firm and write him a letter.

MONICA cranes, looking for WIDDOWSON.

> MONICA

He's been so kind.

> MILLIE

But if you don't love him?

> MONICA
>
> (*Turning to MILLIE with a worried frown.*) He makes
> me feel it would be the cruelest thing in the world not
> to marry him.

The girls are on their way out of the Tate Gallery.

Pausing in the press of people, MONICA is arrested by the sight of a LARGE PICTURE. *King Cophetus and the Beggar Maid*. The king is aging, with greying whiskers. The girl at his feet is young and beautiful.

MONICA gazes at the picture. MILLIE, ahead, comes back and pulls MONICA by the coat.

They walk to the exit – MONICA's mind full of the picture.

EXT. TATE GALLERY – DAY

On the steps outside, MONICA looks round briefly, but there is no sign of WIDDOWSON.

MILLIE notices this, and also looks round for him. They descend the steps, arm in arm.

> MONICA
>
> Dear Millie!

They run down the steps together, in a sudden rush of high spirits and laughter. They walk away together.

Then MILLIE crosses the road, away from MONICA, and catches a BUS. MONICA takes a last look behind. No WIDDOWSON.

She sets off, walking briskly.

EXT. POOR TERRACE – CLAPHAM – DAY

MONICA approaches the door of a SMALL HOUSE in a dingy row. She knocks. There is no response. She frowns slightly in surprise and knocks again.

A slight pause, then VIRGINIA comes to the door. She looks flushed, and her eyes are wide.

> MONICA
>
> What is it? (*She crosses the threshold, and turns back.*) What's the matter?

But VIRGINIA cannot answer. She indicates for MONICA to proceed. MONICA goes down the dreary passage.

INT. POKY LITTLE SITTING ROOM – DAY

MONICA enters the sitting room, followed by VIRGINIA.

ALICE is by the fireplace, a glazed smile on her face.

On the one good chair, his hat on his knee, sits WIDDOWSON.

MONICA is shocked. She looks from one to the other.

ALICE smiles blissfully.

> VIRGINIA
>
> My dear …

MONICA turns to VIRGINIA, her face wary with fright.

> VIRGINIA
>
> (*Gentle and tremulous*) Oh, darling Monica … !

> ALICE
>
> Dear, dear girl!

Transfixed, MONICA can say nothing.

INT. MONICA'S BEDROOM – NIGHT

MILLIE pokes her head round the door.

MILLIE

Feeling better?

HER POV: MONICA in bed. The room is full of flowers – roses, sweetpeas, and lily-of-the-valley.

MONICA

(*She has lost her voice*) A little.

MILLIE enters and puts a parcel on her lap. MONICA looks down at it for a moment, then opens it. It is a beautiful LOCKET on a chain.

MILLIE

There are more flowers downstairs.

MONICA looks beleaguered, her face small and pale against the pillow.

INT. THE TYPEWRITER SCHOOLROOM – DAY

The GIRLS, assembled for MARY's speech, chatter. There is a hush as MARY enters and steps on to the platform. She looks about her for RHODA, and is upset to see RHODA is not there. But, as she begins, RHODA enters and stands quietly at the back.

MARY

Last week, I received a letter from an unemployed
clerk abusing me for encouraging female competition.
He was rude and hostile, and someone with whom
it was impossible to argue, so I didn't reply. But
there are many who would agree with him and tell
us that not only are we unsexing ourselves, but we
are depriving men of their livelihoods, and thus
damaging women by attacking their protectors. I

say they are wrong. I say that women have the right to work. To a livelihood, and to independence. This right is already accepted in a few spheres. Women should undertake womanly occupations, I'm told: Why don't I train girls as nurses or governesses? I have nothing against these callings. But we can't all be nurses and governesses. And, in any case, they hinder rather than help us in our struggle. They are the ghettos to which men would confine us. We must expand into other spheres. If we are to realise ourselves as mature human beings we must pursue our claims. To be honest, I don't care if we push men out or not. I don't care what the result is, so long as women are made strong and self-reliant. When I think of the wretched existence of most women, I'm tempted to say ... Let the world perish rather than that things should go on as they are. (*Her voice breaks momentarily.*) So, our threatened and disaffected clerk must do the best he can for himself. He is suffering for the stupidity of men of all ages. It isn't our fault. We don't wish to cause hardship. But we will not continue to suffer! We intend to become a new species. We intend to be active. Have active lives. Retaining the old virtues but adding those that have been thought appropriate only for men. We can be gentle ... but we must also be strong. We can live decent lives. But we must be instructed in the ways of the world, nonetheless. Whether women equal men, I neither know nor care. We aren't their equal in size, weight, muscle power – in brain power, for all I know. Nor do I care. That has nothing to do with it. It's enough for us to know that our natural growth has been stunted. We intend to fight for our rights.

Let responsibility for disorder rest on those who have been the cause of it. We must be prepared to pay any cost ... any cost, to free ourselves from the yoke of patronage and self-contempt that we have inherited. Thank you.

The GIRLS rise, clapping.

MARY nods and smiles, then returns to her office with a quick step.

The GIRLS, very stimulated, talk as they leave together in a hubbub of sound.

INT. OFFICE – DAY

RHODA enters the office quietly. MARY turns. They regard each other, and embrace with fervour.

                    RHODA
        I've been an ill-mannered pig.

They embrace again.

                    MARY
        (Into RHODA's shoulder) No, no. So have I.

A KNOCK on the door.

                    MARY
        Yes?

MONICA puts a nervous head round the door.

                    MONICA
        May I ... ?

                    MARY
        (Expansive) Of course. Come in!

MARY sweeps a pile of books from the spare upright chair for MONICA to take a seat. But MONICA remains standing by the door.

MARY

Rhoda says you're doing splendidly.

MONICA

(*Her eyes down*) Thank you.

They wait for her to speak. She forces herself to look up.

MONICA

I'm ... It ... I'm afraid I shall be leaving.

The two women look at each other, and then at MONICA, in surprise.

MONICA

I'm going to be married.

RHODA turns her head sharply. She gazes at MONICA with a look of glowing savagery. MONICA pales, then returns the stare, her chin up mutinously.

MARY

My dear! May we know his name?

MONICA

(*Still looking at RHODA*) Edmund Widdowson.

MARY

A friend of the family?

MONICA

My sisters know him, yes.

MARY

I see. What does he do?

MONICA breaks away from RHODA's stare and turns to MARY.

MONICA

He is of independent means.

MARY

Ah.

She looks briefly at RHODA in relief. He sounds like a gentleman.

RHODA sits on the edge of the desk, her manner interrogatory.

RHODA

How long have you known him?

MONICA hesitates.

RHODA

How long?

MONICA

For some time.

MARY

When did you ... ?

MONICA

I'm afraid I shall be leaving at once. My ... fiancé ...
wishes the marriage to ...

Despite herself, she falters. RHODA and MARY exchange a glance.
There is something wrong here.

MARY

My dear, are you certain?

MONICA looks at her with a stiff expression.

MARY

Is there any rush? Why not wait? At least finish your
training.

MONICA

It's not as though I'm any good at it.

RHODA

Nonsense.

MARY

We look upon you as one of our brightest prospects.

MONICA looks up at the glowering RHODA.

MONICA

I'm not a fighter, Rhoda. Not in your way.

RHODA

Then learn to be.

MONICA

Perhaps it's a family weakness. I can't bear
dissension.

RHODA

But, without it, we cannot . . .

MONICA

I have to think of my sisters.

RHODA

You mean, you're . . .

MARY

(*Together*) But you can't . . .

MONICA

What sort of future is there for them? What sort of
life? They act as though they've no right to a space on
this earth! I can't bear it.

RHODA

And that's precisely why . . .

MONICA

They don't know how to fight. A raised voice makes
them tremble. They haven't the taste for friction. (*A
slight pause.*) He has agreed to provide for them. To
give them a home with us.

MARY

Won't that be a burden?

MONICA

(*Eyes down*) He's ... very well-placed.

Silence.

RHODA

How old is this paragon?

MONICA

(*Looks at RHODA honestly*) He's forty-eight.

And RHODA's look, in return, is also honest. All is clear. The girl is
sacrificing herself for all the wrong reasons.

RHODA

(*Gentle*) My dear, you can't. You don't know what
you're doing.

MONICA looks at her with brave resignation.

RHODA

You don't know what you're doing. There are other
solutions, believe me. Trust me, Monica. You're not
a child. Poverty isn't the only prison in life. Why
burden men with the responsibility for our welfare?
We need ... We must ... We have to grow up.

MONICA turns her face away.

RHODA

It's no more than the vilest commerce. Do you love
him?

MONICA

He's been so kind. (*Turning back to RHODA*) Yes. Yes,
I do. He's made me love him.

RHODA looks at MARY, who gives her a shrewd, pensive look,
which says: 'Are you competent to deal with this? What do you
know about love?'

RHODA

(*Resolved*). I see. Well. In that case, we've no right to
say any more. If it is a question of love … (*Glancing
at MARY, defiantly*) I daresay we've no right to
interfere.

RHODA crosses the room, puts her hand on MONICA's shoulder,
and leaves the office. MONICA looks after her in pensive sadness.

MARY

Rhoda's very fond of you. (*Then she smiles*) I'm afraid
you haven't enjoyed the work here.

MONICA smiles ruefully.

MARY

Too dry?

They both laugh.

MARY

Ye-es, it is a problem.

MARY sees MONICA out.

> MARY

You must begin to make plans for your new life. Do call on us for any assistance you may need with arrangements. We'll be delighted to help.

EXT. SUBURBAN CHURCH – DAY

A crash of BELLS as PEOPLE arrive for the wedding.

VIRGINIA and ALICE hurry along the path, smiling and happy, followed by RHODA and MARY, elegant in new clothes.

WIDDOWSON arrives, accompanied by an older, desiccated FRIEND – his best man. They all go in the church.

A CARRIAGE arrives and stops. EVERARD (who is to give her away) emerges, and helps MONICA out, who is almost drowning in a voluminous, white wedding dress.

She smiles, grateful for his moral support.

INT. CHURCH VESTRY – DAY

MILLIE, the bridesmaid, waits in the vestry. MONICA and EVERARD arrive and arrange themselves.

The ORGAN MUSIC changes.

INT. CHURCH – DAY

ORGAN MUSIC.

MONICA and EVERARD walk down the aisle, making a handsome couple. The VICAR, at the altar, and the WEDDING GUESTS in the pews, watch them.

MONICA catches RHODA's eye, and gives her a little, strained smile.

At the altar, WIDDOWSON turns to greet his bride. He cannot believe she is here, beside him. He looks at her, frowning in an attempt to compose himself. Her face is tense but composed.

The ORGAN MUSIC stops and the VICAR steps forward.

INT. DRAWING ROOM – WIDDOWSON'S HOUSE – DAY

A large room with French windows overlooking a garden.

The wedding reception is underway. MONICA moves about, talking to the GUESTS. WIDDOWSON, speaking to MARY BARFOOT, keeps an eye on MONICA as she approaches EVERARD – who is talking to VIRGINIA and ALICE.

                    VIRGINIA
        We were just saying . . .

                    ALICE
        (*Together*) So kind . . .

                    VIRGINIA
        To act in loco parentis . . .

                    EVERARD
        Not at all. An extremely amiable duty.

He and MONICA exchange a mischievous smile.

ON: WIDDOWSON. His face darkens. He hears nothing that MARY says.

NEW ANGLE: RHODA and MILLIE stand together.

                    MILLIE
        (*As they watch MONICA*) She looks lovely, does she
        not?

                    RHODA
        Yes. Yes. Yes.

RHODA puts down her plate and walks away. MILLIE looks after her with a wry smile.

RHODA prowls. EVERARD appears at her side. He indicates ... does she want her glass refilled? She shakes her head.

At the same moment, they both notice WIDDOWSON, standing with his BEST MAN, looking miserable in midst of the noisy throng.

As if in mutual consent, RHODA and EVERARD turn together and stroll out into the garden.

ON: WIDDOWSON.

> WIDDOWSON
>
> How much longer does this go on?

> BEST MAN
>
> (*He clutches his notes for his speech.*) About another
> hour, I think.

WIDDOWSON groans.

A plump, fashionably-dressed woman has introduced herself to MARY. This is MRS LUKE WIDDOWSON.

> MRS LUKE WIDDOWSON
>
> ... I was married to his poor brother.

She smiles encouragingly across at WIDDOWSON, and gives him a wave. She gets a gloomy look back. MRS LUKE sighs, and cranes to look at MONICA, who is talking animatedly to a group of her TYPING SCHOOL FRIENDS.

> MRS LUKE
>
> At least she's a pretty little thing.

> MARY
>
> Oh, more than that.

MRS LUKE

He never gave me the least notion. I said to him:
Edmund, if you'd only told me you wanted to marry,
I could have found you a girl with means. A decent
background. Good family.

MARY bows slightly, excusing herself.

MRS LUKE

(*Left alone*) Oh dear.

Nothing daunted, she turns to ALICE and VIRGINIA.

MRS LUKE

I hear the wedding presents are in the morning room.

The sisters escort her away eagerly.

NEW ANGLE: The animated sound of talk rises.

The BEST MAN threads his way to the wedding table, and taps a
glass for silence.

MRS LUKE persuades MONICA and WIDDOWSON together for
the speeches. ALICE beams in pure happiness. VIRGINIA nods,
smiling, as a maid refills her glass. The BEST MAN cannot quell
the sound.

EVERARD, coming in from the garden with RHODA, steps to the
end of the long table.

EVERARD

Ladies and gentlemen ... Ladies and gentlemen ...
As it was my great pleasure to be asked today to
give away the bride ... with reluctance. May I, on
behalf of the newly-married couple, thank you all
for being so kind as to be with us today. I know that
Monica particularly wishes me to thank those of you
who have travelled to be here. And may I, on behalf

of the guests, wish you, Monica, and you, Edmund, the greatest good wishes from us all. (*He raises his glass.*)

Cheers.

EVERARD

I now call upon the best man.

Cheers.

BEST MAN

(*Fiddling with his notes*) I ... I ... (*He loses a piece of paper, then retrieves it.*)

Cheers.

BEST MAN

Ladies and gentlemen ... What? Oh, thank you. I'm afraid ... (*He launches into his prepared speech.*) It was the well-known poet, Gervase Burt, who said, did he not, 'The lovebirds perching in the tree, Feel less inspired than me for thee.' Gazing, as we do today, at ...

A WAITER intrudes with a huge knife for the cake cutting.

BEST MAN

I beg your pardon. (*He loses his place*) ... walking through life's garden together, we wish them the joy of that great poem: 'a garden is a lovesome thing, God wot, Fringed grove ... ferned grot.' May your future path together be fringed and, ah, ferned ... I ... ah ...

RHODA attempts to mask her giggles. EVERARD looks down at her, delighted by her sense of humour.

MRS LUKE

Never mind, Mr Newdick. Splendid! Cut the cake,
Edmund.

WIDDOWSON gives her a look of dislike but moves behind the cake
obediently and picks up the knife. MONICA moves to his side, puts
her hand over his, and they cut the cake.

Applause. Shouts of 'Kiss the bride.'

WIDDOWSON, awkward, pecks MONICA on the cheek, and MONICA
flinches slightly.

RHODA and EVERARD both register this, and turn to each other.
EVERARD looks at MONICA with a new alertness.

INT. RHODA'S BEDROOM – NIGHT

RHODA, in her dressing gown, hangs up the dress she wore at the
wedding. She takes down her hair, and looks at herself in the glass.
She looks on the shelves for a book, picking up more than one. But
she is restless. She prowls, picking up a hairbrush, and playing
with the ornaments on her dressing table.

DISSOLVE TO: EVERARD chatting at the Wedding.

ON: RHODA, unable to decipher her mood, she throws herself down
on the bed. Turning her head, she can see herself in the mirror.
She leans on her elbow, looking at herself. She pushes her hair up,
turns her head, looking at the angle of her neck.

She lies back, hands behind her head, thinking about how it would
be to have an affair with EVERARD BARFOOT.

EXT. ESPLANADE AND PORT – GUERNSEY – DAY

The sun is shining. The sea sparkles.

A FISHING BOAT comes alongside the jetty, watched by WELL-DRESSED VISITORS.

On the esplanade, PEOPLE are promenading majestically in their best clothes and fine hats.

One of the strolling couples is MONICA and WIDDOWSON.

They turn a corner, with a last glimpse of her skirt.

EXT. LITTLE STREET – DAY

WIDDOWSON and MONICA stroll along the little street. He grasps her arm tightly, proud in his pale, summer suit. She looks enchanting in blue and white, as she bends to fondle a SMALL DOG.

WIDDOWSON's eyes are full of wonder at her. He offers her his arm as she straightens up – moving gently, as though the dream will shatter if he moves too violently.

She smiles at him, and takes his arm cheerfully.

INT. HOTEL BEDROOM – DUSK

MONICA is at the dressing table, finishing her toilette before going down to dinner. As she puts down her hair-brush, WIDDOWSON appears behind her.

He puts an opal choker about her neck.

>   MONICA
> Oh Edmund!

Her eyes widen as she gazes at herself in the glass, WIDDOWSON at her shoulder. She touches the choker, her mouth slightly open. He broods over her like a dark stain.

EXT. SEASIDE – DAY

MONICA and WIDDOWSON are on the beach.

MONICA climbs over the rocks, jumping easily from rock to rock, avoiding the pools. She turns to laugh at him as he tries, less successfully, to do the same.

She begins to climb higher, scrambling with agility. He pauses, taking his hat off for a second, puffing. She calls down to him – the sound muffled by the waves.

He squints up at her, not hearing what she said. She gestures, waving him on. Obediently, he scrambles up after her.

EXT. ANOTHER PART OF THE SEASIDE – DAY

From above, we see them sitting on a sandy ledge, looking at the sea below them.

MONICA is lying back, her large straw hat on the rock beside her.

He sits, more formally, his back against the rocks.

We see them closer. She leans sideways, laughing, in a teasing mood, beyond his Easter Island profile.

> MONICA
> You do! You do! (*Her voice sounds like the cry of a seabird.*)

> WIDDOWSON
> Not at all.

EXT. ANOTHER PART OF THE SEASIDE – DAY – LATER

WIDDOWSON helps her across the lower rocks.

> WIDDOWSON
> I take life seriously when it is necessary . . .

MONICA

But that shouldn't be all the time.

INT. HOTEL DINING ROOM – NIGHT

WIDDOWSON

Not at all.

MONICA and WIDDOWSON are having dinner. He is looking at the wine bottle proffered by the WAITER. He nods his head.

WIDDOWSON

I'm enjoying myself now, aren't I?

MONICA

In a grave sort of way.

She smiles at him, and her attention is diverted to a table across the room where a group of YOUNG PEOPLE laugh merrily.

There is a handsome middle-aged woman, (MRS COSGROVE) – THREE YOUNG WOMEN, all well-dressed, and a YOUNG MAN with bright fair hair. They lean across the table, teasing one another.

WIDDOWSON

Nonsense. I haven't a care in the world.

MONICA

(*Returning her attention to him.*) Yes, but when we get home ... ?

WIDDOWSON

How do you mean?

MONICA

We will see people?

WIDDOWSON

What people?

MONICA looks at him in covert alarm.

He removes the napkin ring from his napkin with careful precision, and arranges the napkin on his lap, as the WAITER appears with the soup.

MONICA's eyes stray again to the happy group across the room.

EXT. HOTEL RECEPTION ROOM – DAY

It's raining.

VIEW THROUGH the rain-washed reception room window. MONICA, blurred, and seated next to WIDDOWSON, is looking out the window. WIDDOWSON is reading a book.

INT. HOTEL RECEPTION ROOM – SAME TIME – DAY

ON: WIDDOWSON, holding up his book in order to see it properly.

A PAGE-BOY lolls at the reception counter. MONICA, at his side, moves restlessly, her book in her lap.

> WIDDOWSON
>
> Don't you care for it?

> MONICA
>
> I'm sorry?

> WIDDOWSON
>
> The Walter Scott.

She looks down at her book.

> MONICA
>
> Oh. Yes. (*She glances out of the window at the rain.*)

> WIDDOWSON
>
> (*Following her glance.*) We were right to postpone our
> walk.

MONICA

Yes.

WIDDOWSON

You don't want to go out in the rain with that silly crowd, do you?

She doesn't reply.

WIDDOWSON

I've been thinking. We might move on. To Jersey.

MONICA smiles and waves as MRS COSGROVE and her PARTY, wrapped against the weather, cross the hall, laughing and talking, break the silence.

MONICA

It certainly might be livelier. (*Slight pause*) Mrs Cosgrove has asked us to a musical evening. (*She puts on a bright expression.*)

WIDDOWSON puts down his book. His face is black.

MONICA

Did I mention that she is a neighbour of Miss Barfoot's? She lives in Chelsea. Quite close. Edmund? Shall we go?

WIDDOWSON

I think not.

MONICA

Oh? Why?

WIDDOWSON

I think, dear little wife, that you must agree to leave these decisions to me.

MONICA

But I should like to. We can't always be on our own
together.

WIDDOWSON

(*He returns to his book, flicking a page.*) Why not?

MONICA

But surely . . .

WIDDOWSON

I need no other companion. Neither should you.

MONICA

But I should like to go.

WIDDOWSON

No.

MONICA

Why not?

WIDDOWSON

Because I forbid it.

In a childlike rage, MONICA leaves the table and sweeps across
the room, her shawl slipping from her shoulders to the floor.
Embarrassed, he follows her, picking up the shawl.

Halfway up the stairs, she turns and sees him. He joins her on the
landing and hands her the shawl. She refuses to take it, giving him
a look of flashing defiance, and marches up the stairs.

WIDDOWSON

(*Following her*) You . . . left it on your chair.

INT. HOTEL BEDROOM – DAY

MONICA enters the hotel bedroom. WIDDOWSON follows behind
her, still clutching the shawl. He puts it down awkwardly on a
chair. She turns away, refusing to speak to him.

> WIDDOWSON
> (Lame) It . . . it's always advisable to be orderly. Then
> nothing goes astray.

She turns with a dark, mutinous face.

INT. HALLWAY AND DRAWING ROOM – FINE HOUSE – NIGHT

The Musical Evening.

In the hallway of a pleasant house, the HOSTESS, a plump, smiling
woman, greets MRS COSGROVE, her DAUGHTER, young MR BEVIS
and his TWO SISTERS.

They move into the drawing room, which is full of PEOPLE, mostly
young, with MOTHERS and FATHERS, and ELDERLY AUNTS
sitting at the side. A group of YOUNG WOMEN cluster around the
piano where a SATURNINE YOUNG MAN is playing Chopin with
feeling.

There is enthusiastic applause, especially from the young women.

The PIANIST shakes his locks and flares his nostrils, thrilling
them even more.

> HOSTESS
> (As the noise subsides) Thank you. There will now be
> refreshments.

The hall door is opened by the BUTLER. MONICA and WIDDOWSON
enter. She looks even more beautiful in white, the opal choker at
her neck. WIDDOWSON looks like a dog who has been whipped

and feels murderous. His eyes dart about … he is appalled by the throng of people.

The HOSTESS moves forward with a smile to greet them.

> HOSTESS
>
> Delighted – do come in.

MRS COSGROVE breaks away from a group and comes to join in the welcome, her handsome face in a warmly welcoming smile, her hand outstretched.

MONICA joins her and is spirited into the room, leaving WIDDOWSON stranded.

The HOSTESS waves her hand, and the hubbub of conversation dies.

> HOSTESS
>
> Miss Bevis will now sing for us.

MISS BEVIS steps to the piano. The PIANIST sits. They consult the sheet music briefly. MISS BEVIS takes her stand.

Then she sings a *Schubert* song. Her voice is true and sweet.

The young women are affected. One YOUNG MAN dares to grasp a hand. MONICA sits, bright-eyed, enjoying herself. She gets up and moves about the room, enjoying the dresses. The MUSIC begins to affect her. It has a melancholy feel. She looks briefly at her husband, who stands by the door, his hands behind his back, chin up, seemingly made of wood. Her glance moves to another group … to a YOUNG GIRL bending her head as a fresh-faced BOY whispers in her ear.

MONICA looks down in her lap.

INT. DRAWING ROOM – NIGHT – LATER

The PIANIST plays for dancing.

MONICA, seated, next to her husband, watches. She is asked to dance by the YOUNG MAN. She looks at her husband. His look is strange and bright, his smile fixed.

She gives him her gloves and fan, and joins the dance.

WIDDOWSON holds the gloves and fan in clenched hands, and watches her. The lighting gives his eyes a strange, pale effect.

MONICA, dancing, forgets him. She laughs, and weaves her way through the dance gracefully, back among her own kind – young men and women of her own age.

MRS COSGROVE, with an astute glance, notices WIDDOWSON, and moves to him. She tries to speak, but he only has eyes for MONICA, who weaves back again in the dance, her face alight with pleasure.

INT. HOTEL BEDROOM – NIGHT

WIDDOWSON is in his dressing gown. She is undressing after the evening out.

> WIDDOWSON
> My wishes were clearly known to you ...

> MONICA
> I must have some freedom! What's wrong to want to enjoy oneself? If you had wished to go, you wouldn't have needed _my_ permission.

> WIDDOWSON
> Of course not. I'm a man.

> MONICA
> (_Pauses in the act of putting on her negligée_) You mean that I ... must obey you ... in everything?

WIDDOWSON

Of course! Otherwise, there's no sense to the world.

MONICA, stunned, sits down at the dressing table, grasps her hair-brush without thinking, and tries to clear her thoughts.

MONICA

But surely ... love must be free?

WIDDOWSON

(*In a low, threatening voice*) What do you mean?

MONICA

For love to exist it must be taken on trust. Freely
given.

WIDDOWSON

I see. You mean if I exercise my rights as a husband,
you'll cease to love me. Is that it?

MONICA

Of course not!

His woeful face, setting into its old, depressed folds, upsets her. She flies to his side.

WIDDOWSON

All those people! I hate it. You must promise ...

MONICA

Edmund! You're hurting me.

WIDDOWSON

Promise you'll be faithful.

MONICA

Faithful? What do you mean?

WIDDOWSON

I can't bear to see you with them.

She breaks away.

WIDDOWSON

Will you promise? If I allow you to ...

MONICA

(*Blazing*) Allow? Allow me? I'm to be some sort of
slave?

WIDDOWSON

Please ... (*He tries to embrace her.*)

MONICA

No! I won't have it! I won't be treated like ...

He grabs her fiercely and holds her tight.

WIDDOWSON

Don't leave me! I'll agree. Whatever you say. But don't
leave me. Say you love me.

MONICA

Of course I love you.

She tries to pull away, but he holds onto her ineptly, fearing to tear
her negligée.

WIDDOWSON

You're my wife. You don't know what it's like when
you aren't with me! When you leave the room I think
you don't exist. I can't believe ... I watch you when
you're asleep. I still can't believe that you belong to
me.

MONICA

Please don't upset yourself.

WIDDOWSON

Say you love me!

He grips her so fiercely that she cries out. She tries again to pull
away, but he holds her tightly.

WIDDOWSON

Say you love me. Put your arms round my neck.
Please.

She puts her arms around his neck.

WIDDOWSON

No, closer. Hold on to me. Don't leave me. Go on, say it.
Say you love me!

She kisses his forehead.

WIDDOWSON

Can't you say it? Say you love me, please. Please.

He holds her so tightly that she begins to gasp, unable to breathe.
She starts to struggle, involuntarily.

WIDDOWSON

You must love me. You must! You must . . . you must
love me. Love me I tell you!

Then he cracks her across the face.

They are both terribly shaken. She stumbles back from him,
knocking over a chair, a hand to her face, her eyes full of tears from
the pain of the blow. He groans loudly – almost a bellow of shock.

He throws himself on his knees before her.

WIDDOWSON

Oh . . . oh, no, please . . . What have I done? Please.
Don't make me behave like this! What am I doing?
You must love me. Please . . . please, you must love me,
please . . .

He groans and mutters, clutching at her bare legs, grovelling, and kissing her feet. She gazes down at him, her eyes wide with fright, in utter confusion as to what has happened.

She pulls away from him, with a vague instinct, holding onto the furniture to keep her balance.

He holds onto her legs, moving forward on his knees.

                    WIDDOWSEN
        Please … please – oh, please … say you love me. Say
        you love me … please!!

Again, the animal groan, lower, rumbling in his throat.

It frightens her, and she looks in anguish at the door. But he clutches, and mumbles, and she remains in the centre of the room.

She looks down at the top of his head as he mutters into the skirt of her negligée.

Her face begins to show distaste. Trapped, unable to move, her eyes betray an increasing objectivity.

Fade out.

Fade in.

EXT. FOGGY LONDON STREETS – DAY

PEDESTRIANS are blundering about in the fog.

INT. DINING ROOM – MARY'S HOUSE – NIGHT

RHODA, elegant in a red blouse, has finished having dinner with EVERARD.

IDA, the maid, clearing the dessert plates, hovers over the place set for Mary. She looks at RHODA in enquiry.

RHODA

I don't think she's coming, Ida. (*Looks at watch*)
Perhaps a tray later, if necessary.

IDA bobs, smiles, then goes.

EVERARD

I doubt we shall see Mary tonight. I lost my way
several times in the park.

RHODA

You came across the park? In the fog?

EVERARD

Almost walked into the round pond. (*Grins*)

RHODA

Mary's bound to want to sit with Tom as long as
possible.

EVERARD

My brother's a lucky man. If anyone can revive him,
she can. I once told Mary she should volunteer to
walk the hospital wards. Just seeing her would have
the sick and the lame rising from their beds.

RHODA looks at him, wondering if he's being sarcastic.

INT. DRAWING ROOM – NIGHT

Nice lighting. A seductive atmosphere. The fire in the fireplace
crackles.

A bottle of port is on a side-table. They are both drinking.

RHODA puts down her glass and takes a cigar from a box.

EVERARD lights it for her.

EVERARD

No, on the contrary. I'm a fervent admirer of your
single-minded vigour. I intend to acquire some.

She sits, putting her feet up characteristically on the sofa.

RHODA

Oh? On whose behalf?

EVERARD

My own. Self-improvement!

RHODA

Bravo.

EVERARD

I shall, of course, need your assistance.

She gives him an ironic look through the smoke of the cigar.

EVERARD

You know that I live alone?

RHODA

Naturally.

EVERARD

Anything but natural ...

He gets up and sits down beside her.

EVERARD

... for a man in love.

RHODA

Are you asking me to be your confidant?

EVERARD

No.

She looks at him, then turns away. She plays with the ash in the tray.

RHODA

I see. (*She turns to face him.*) I see. (*She rises*) Well, I trust you soon recover.

But she is agitated. She moves and rings the BELL.

He watches her. Is she going to throw him out?

IDA enters, with cups, a coffee pot and two small jugs on a tray.

RHODA

Thank you, Ida. Coffee?

IDA leaves.

RHODA

Milk?

EVERARD shakes his head.

RHODA

Cream? Sugar?

He crosses, with an ominous expression, and takes the cup.

EVERARD

You don't take me seriously.

RHODA

Should I?

The CUP she is holding shakes a little.

EVERARD

Allow me. (*He takes her cup, sets it down, and sits beside her.*)

(The next two lines are spoken together:)

RHODA

I think we'd better ...

EVERARD

Are you going to allow me to ... ?

A slight hiatus.

EVERARD

You'd better let me go on. I'll try not to be too
ridiculous.

He gets up and walks about, jingling the change in his pocket. He
is in no hurry – making her nervous.

EVERARD

(*Almost plaintive*) The fact is ... I'm finding it hard to
do without you.

They exchange a covert glance – just missing each other.

EVERARD

I've no money. And I don't intend to make any. I've no
ambition in that direction. So, you see, I've nothing to
offer. Except the freedom for us both to live our own
lives without restraint.

She remains turned away from him.

EVERARD

However, there is something I must make clear. It is
love I'm asking for.

At the word 'love,' she looks at him briefly. He waits for a response,
but she crosses to an armchair and sits, twisting her fingers.

EVERARD

Do you not think it possible – a love between a man
and a woman intelligent enough to understand the
need for freedom on both sides?

She looks up with a stiff little smile.

EVERARD

Well?

There is a long pause. She won't return his gaze. He stands over
her.

RHODA

I believe it's customary to give thanks for such an
offer. Isn't that what the novels say? So, 'thank you.'

She gives him a prim little smile. He grabs a small chair, swings it
dangerously in the air, then plants it beside her and sits, grasping
her hand so tightly that she flinches.

EVERARD

(*Mutters*) Stop it. D'you want me to make you
understand what it means when a man says he loves
you? Eh?

She tries to get away, but he pinions her arms, and looks down at
her face, perusing it in wonder.

EVERARD

It's so odd. When we met, I didn't think of you as a
woman.

He kisses her. The kiss is not prolonged, nor particularly
passionate. But, when we see her face, it is dazed. As if she'd
received a blow.

EVERARD perceives that, despite herself, she is responsive.

EVERARD

(*He lets her go.*) Ah, yes. I think you should tell me
what you feel – don't you?

RHODA speaks as though her voice is hurting her.

RHODA

I'm afraid the answer must be no. For one thing, I
don't love you. And ...

EVERARD

Well?

RHODA

I cannot be involved in anything that interferes with
my work.

EVERARD

Teaching girls to type? Waste of time. They're all
going to marry and have babies.

RHODA

You suggest we live together, and you know nothing
at all about me!

She is blazing, and this makes him desire her. There is a tussle.
He enjoys being sadistic with her. And there is something in her
that responds.

He laughs, which angers her. She turns, tripping on her skirt, her
hair falls down. He catches her in his arms.

EVERARD

(*Grinning*) What can you do? Against the barbarian?

RHODA

I don't pretend to have your brute strength.

He holds her for a second, then lets her go. She pins up her hair.

RHODA

Will you go away?

He looks at her amiably and walks to the curtains, which he draws, revealing a wall of fog.

RHODA

I can't force you to go.

EVERARD

Oh, please … do sit down. I promise not to attack you.
For the present.

To prove his point, he sits at a distance, adjusting the line of his trousers.

EVERARD

Sit down, you might as well.

But she puts her hand on the door handle.

EVERARD

Please – don't go!

Something needful in his voice makes her pause. She crosses and sits at a distance.

RHODA

I have no intention of marrying. Ever.

EVERARD

That doesn't mean you have to be celibate.

RHODA

My work gives me all the satisfaction I need.

EVERARD

I can't say I applaud the sacrifice.

RHODA

Now we come to the male derision.

                    EVERARD

You find chastity a virtue? I had expected more
courage.

                    RHODA

(*Ringing the bell*) I'll see if they can find you a cab.

She goes out into the hall. He follows, amiably.

INT. HALL – MARY'S HOUSE – NIGHT

IDA appears in response to the bell. RHODA speaks to her. IDA
disappears below.

EVERARD takes his coat and stick.

                    EVERARD

 Will you think of me?

RHODA's face darkens at his insolent assurance. She smiles at him
faintly, as at a runner who has come last.

INT. CONSERVATORY – MARY'S HOUSE – MORNING

MARY lifts the cover of the entrée dish at the breakfast table.

                    MARY

 Mmm. Scrambled eggs!

She helps herself liberally.

                    MARY

 I was too tired to eat last night. But Tom's looking
 better.

                    RHODA

 Splendid.

RHODA sits opposite, drinking from a large French bowl of coffee
with both hands.

RHODA

What time did you get in?

MARY

Past midnight. I imagine you saw nothing of Everard?

RHODA

No, I did. He was here.

MARY

Really? How long did he stay?

RHODA

Till midnight.

MARY

(*Surprised*) He shouldn't have waited. I'm surprised I got back at all.

RHODA, coffee bowl cupped, watches MARY eat.

RHODA

What was it about? The scandal. Your cousin losing his inheritance ...

MARY

Must you know?

RHODA

Yes. Your cousin is pleased to imagine himself in love with me.

The shock to MARY is terrible. She recovers with difficulty. She puts her cup down carefully.

MARY

Has he ... (*Clears her throat*) ... has he asked you to marry him?

RHODA

No.

MARY's relief is visible, although she prudently turns her face from RHODA. No longer hungry, she pushes her plate away, and rises, brushing the crumbs from her skirt.

RHODA

Are you going to tell me what he did?

MARY

Perhaps you should ask him. (*She changes her mind.*) Very well. We used to know some people in Oxford. Everard and I went there regularly to stay. They were ... progressive. They believed in mixing.

RHODA

Mixing?

MARY

Encouraging people to change class. (*Slight pause*) As it happened, I knew the girl. She served in the local shop.

RHODA

Was she pretty?

MARY

(*Bitterly*) Oh yes. Enchanting.

RHODA

(*After a pause*) Am I to infer the rest?

MARY

When her parents died, it was arranged that she should go to London to live with a married sister. She and Everard happened to share a carriage and ... apparently formed a relationship. When the storm broke, he denied all responsibility, and behaved like ... We couldn't get him to ...

She's unable to continue.

RHODA

You mean he lied?

MARY

He refused to say anything at all. He walked away from the whole affair. Well, that's not quite true. He did make an allowance for the child.

RHODA

(*Her composure shaken*) Child? There was a child?

MARY

Yes. She died a year later. He behaved appallingly. His father couldn't forgive him. (*She makes a half-exasperated sound.*) He asked me, the other day, if you knew. When I said 'partly' he was furious – as though he were perfectly innocent.

RHODA

You knew the girl?

MARY

Oh yes.

RHODA turns, and picks up her books from the chair.

RHODA

Well, what does it matter?

MARY, stung, turns to answer. But IDA appears at the door, her eyes wide, a telegram in her hand.

IDA

(*Alarmed*) A telegram, Miss Mary!

MARY takes the telegram, opens it, reads the message and sits abruptly.

> RHODA

Bad news. (*It is hardly a question.*)

MARY, unable to answer, gives her the telegram, and hurries out, on the verge of tears.

INT. DRAWING ROOM – DAY

RHODA is cradling MARY in her arms.

> MARY

I can't ... I ... (*She looks up into RHODA's face, her voice full of surprised discovery.*) I can't bear it!

> RHODA

(*Shocked and white-faced*) Sssh!

> MARY

Tom! I loved him! You didn't know him ... ah ... (*She recovers slightly*) He ... (*then, with a sudden, cold clarity*) I can't bear it.

EXT. LAWYER'S CHAMBERS – DAY

CLERKS and YOUNG MESSENGERS go in and come out, and pass, papers in hand.

INT. LAWYER'S CHAMBERS – DAY

In the outer office, SEVEN CLERKS are working, heads bent. One is using a typewriter, clacking away in the corner, watched by an admiring OFFICE BOY. All of the employees are men.

EVERARD enters, ushering in MARY, and his sister-in-law, LILLY – both of them dressed in mourning.

An ELDERLY CLERK escorts them into the lawyer's office, as CLERKS move deferentially out of the way.

EXT. COURTYARD GARDEN – LAWYER'S CHAMBERS – DAY

In the beautifully-kept courtyard garden, SPARROWS peck eagerly at crumbs on the lawn. They are bright-eyed, full of life, lifting, wheeling, and quarrelling over the breadcrumbs.

VIEW THROUGH a window into the Lawyer's Office.

INT. LAWYER'S OFFICE – DAY

The LAWYER, at his desk, is concluding his reading of the will.

> LAWYER
> (*Turns over the last page, and pats the will, as of a task properly conducted.*) So, you see, dear Mrs Tom, all has been arranged for your care and protection . . .

ON: LILLY, looking up at him.

> LAWYER
> . . . and for the future of your dear children. Mr Everard, as executor, and minority legatee in your husband's equity, will have full charge of all financial affairs, so that you may rest assured – you are in safe hands.

LILLY nods. She makes to say something, thinks better of it, and rises. The LAWYER comes around his desk and takes her hand.

> LAWYER
> I am always here, Mrs Tom. The slightest cause for concern, Mr Barfoot can be depended on to help you . . .

> LILLY
> I am most grateful. You've been very kind.

She smiles briefly at MARY, who is standing a little apart. For a second the two women share something.

> LILLY
>
> Yes. I should be grateful to be so well-cared for.

> LAWYER
>
> (*With a fatherly smile*) Good day. Never forget that we
> are here to oblige you in every way ...

INT. OUTER OFFICE – DAY

LILLY, MARY and EVERARD walk through the outer office. MARY looks about her alertly, noting all the details, especially the typewriter.

EXT. LAWYER'S CHAMBERS – DAY

LILLY, MARY and EVERARD emerge into the sunlight, and stand on the steps together.

Then EVERARD steps away into the street to hail a hansom cab.

NEW ANGLE: A CAB stops. EVERARD says a few words to the CABDRIVER, then returns to the steps of the Lawyer's Chambers.

ON: LILLY and MARY.

> LILLY
>
> Oh indeed. I am fortunate. Though whether Everard
> intends to stay in this country ... Why couldn't it
> have been him, not Tom! He has no dependents!

MARY turns, and sees EVERARD and the CAB behind him.

She smiles her thanks to him. He nods abruptly, turns, and strides off down the street, his hands in his pockets.

MARY realizes he heard what Lilly said.

INT. THE HOTHOUSE AT KEW – DAY

EVERARD, dressed as before, walks with absent impatience among the huge-leaved plants and the exotic flowers, without seeming to be aware of his surroundings.

A HOLLOW SOUND. The closing of the door at the far end. But it is a GARDENER. He comes and goes.

EVERARD resumes his pacing. Then he sees RHODA as she passes the window outside. He walks swiftly to meet her as she enters and comes towards him along the narrow path between the tall trees and overhanging shrubs.

EVERARD

Thank you for coming.

RHODA

(*Gravely*) I imagine you had some purpose in asking me.

She sees that something is wrong.

EVERARD

Yes. Would you care to walk?

She nods.

He stands back to let her precede him. She looks at the plants pausing briefly. He follows her grimly. They come to a seat and he puts out a hand, indicating they sit, and throws himself down. She sits beside him carefully.

He and looks up at the canopy of leaves above.

EVERARD

I'm going away.

RHODA

Oh?

EVERARD

Yes.

RHODA

May I ask where?

EVERARD

Lilly – Tom's widow – said she wished I'd died instead
of him.

RHODA

She was distraught. Don't take any notice.

EVERARD

I'm taking on the responsibilities, God damn it.
Doesn't she know what a burden that is?

RHODA

And you expect gratitude?

EVERARD

Why not?

RHODA

Perhaps you should ask yourself why dependents so
rarely behave with grace. (*Pause*) How long will you
be away?

He shakes his head. She looks at his bowed profile.

RHODA

I'm sorry. You were close to your brother.

He looks up, but can't answer. She sees he's in distress and her gaze
softens. She tentatively touches the side of his head. He makes a
painful sound, tries to recover, but breaks into tears. She holds
him gently as he cries.

He recovers and looks down at her, wiping away his tears.

She lays her head consolingly on his shoulder.

EVERARD

(*Into her hair.*) You've made a hateful day bearable . . .

She looks up at him. And loves him. The sudden knowledge makes her catch her breath. Her eyes widen. She looks up at him as at some new, strange species as he bends his head and kisses her.

INT. ENTRANCE HALL – WIDDOWSON'S HOUSE – DAY

MONICA, in a pale dress and a straw hat, runs lightly down the stairs, humming to herself. WIDDOWSON comes out of his study below and looks up at her as she descends. His shoulders droop. He looks older. His expression is disgruntled. She sweeps across the hall to him, and pecks him on the cheek.

WIDDOWSON

Where are you off to?

MONICA

Millie and I are shopping in Oxford Street.

WIDDOWSON

Is she not at work?

MONICA

Miss Nunn had given her the afternoon off.

WIDDOWSON

Would you like me to meet you? We could walk across
the park. I should enjoy an outing.

MONICA

Heavens no. You'd be dreadfully bored, you know
what a goose she is.

WIDDOWSON

In that case . . .

She eludes him and reaches the door. He follows her as she goes out, and down the path.

EXT. FRONT PATH – WIDDOWSON'S HOUSE – DAY

WIDDOWSON

(*At the front door, calls*) Don't be late! I won't have the servants kept . . .

MONICA waves, and disappears out of the gate.

WIDDOWSON turns back into the hall.

INT. HALL – WIDDOWSON'S HOUSE – DAY

WIDDOWSON dithers in the empty hall. All is gloom now that MONICA is gone. He wants to go after her, but there's nothing for it but to return to his study.

INT. STUDY – DAY

He enters the study, closes the door, and stands helplessly. Then, pulling himself together, he selects a book from the bookcase and settles down to read. He tries to make sense of the words – but can't do it.

He gets up and goes to the window. HIS POV: the glory of the summer garden. Roses are dropping over the window, soft and lush.

There is a SOFT KNOCK. The ELDERLY MANSERVANT enters, and clears his throat.

WIDDOWSON jumps slightly, and turns.

MANSERVANT

It's the fishmonger, Mr Edmund.

WIDDOWSON

What?

MANSERVANT

The fishmonger. Mrs Edmund wanted a word with
him.

WIDDOWSON

She's not here.

MANSERVANT

Ah. Oh. Well, shall I . . .

WIDDOWSON

(*Violent*) Tell him to go away!

INT. MARY'S CONSERVATORY – DAY

MARY and RHODA are reading in the conservatory on a warm
Saturday afternoon. The wide doors are open. The DOG lies
sprawled on the verandah.

IDA comes in with the post on a tray.

MARY, feeling idle, gestures for her to leave the letters on the table.
MARY lies back among the cushions then looks through the letters.
There is one with a foreign stamp. Her face lights up then falls. It
is addressed to RHODA.

Something makes RHODA look up. MARY leans over and hands her
the letter. RHODA takes it, somewhat consciously. She makes to put
in her pocket, then opens it casually.

A crushed bunch of violets falls from the envelope.

We hear EVERARD's VOICE.

EXT. ITALIAN TOWN CENTRE – DAY

EVERARD is walking with an OLDER MAN in a Panama hat, a well-dressed middle-aged WOMAN of formidable aspect, and TWO YOUNG WOMEN, finely-dressed.

EVERARD pauses with the taller of the young women to look at the façade of a church.

> EVERARD (V/O)
> ... there is more beauty than you can imagine,
> more delight everywhere the eye turns. I find the
> freshness, the audacity of simplicity remarkable
> after London ...

CUT TO:

EVERARD and the YOUNG WOMAN, among a crowd, watch a religious festival pass. A simple, small group with a crudely-painted Madonna swinging dangerously. The LOCAL VILLAGERS staggering under their burden.

The young woman, AGNES BRISSENDEN, turns to EVERARD, and smiles at him from under her parasol.

CUT TO:

> EVERARD (V/O)
> ... you could not fail to be impressed with the ... I was
> so glad to get your letter, alone as I am here ...

EVERARD and AGNES, followed by her SISTER, then her PARENTS, walk in a fine Italian Garden. They pause to look at a fountain and EVERARD notices a DRAGONFLY on the head of a statue.

He joins AGNES and they look out over balustrading at the fine view.

CUT TO:

EVERARD (V/O)

... the sun shines ... the air is full of jasmine and
roses ... and the sound of three beautiful young
women chattering in Italian at the next table.

CUT TO:

EVERARD sitting at a café table in the open, writing a letter. Birds
make a noise in the vines above him – the noise compounded by
the lively chatter of a group of YOUNG WOMEN at a table close by.

EVERARD (V/O)

All of which makes me long to see you. Hear that cool,
intelligent voice. I dream that you are coming across
the piazza towards me. That tomorrow we leave for
Verona, Vicenza ... Padua. Shall we? Can we? Let the
world spin for our amusement? We'll be the losers if
we don't ...

INT. THE ROYAL ACADEMY – DAY

The low buzz of sound of a fashionable gathering.

MR BEVIS is looking at pictures, his catalogue in his hand.
MONICA, a little further off, gazes wistfully at a picture of a
Soldier's Farewell. She sighs, tears herself away from it, and sees
EVERARD entering, across the room. She moves to BEVIS and
whispers in his ear.

He glances at EVERARD, nods, and leaves.

CUT TO:

INT. THE ROYAL ACADEMY – DAY – MOMENTS LATER

Bronzed and handsome, EVERARD looks down at her and offers his hand.

They shake hands cordially.

                    MONICA
          (*As they move away*) How brown you look!

                    EVERARD
          I've been in Italy. (*He looks at her teasingly*) You're
          looking remarkably well. What have you been up to?

                    MONICA
          Nothing, I assure you.

                    EVERARD
          Nothing at all?

                    MONICA
          (*Turning away to look at a picture*) Mr Barfoot, don't
          be a tease.

MR BEVIS is watching her. A look is exchanged between them.

MONICA and EVERARD walk through to the next room, pausing and gazing at the pictures. Again, she looks round and he turns, following her gaze.

                    EVERARD
          Where is your husband?

                    MONICA
          (*As she looks at another picture*) He doesn't care for
          pictures.

EVERARD

(*Looking at another picture, alongside her*) I see.
(*He peers, closer, looking at the brushwork*) Are you
happy in your marriage?

He turns to her, in profile.

MONICA

(*Likewise*) It was a mistake.

He looks at her, perturbed. He takes her arm and they walk
together in silence, no longer at the pictures.

EVERARD

(*Breaking the silence at last*) Do you see Miss Nunn
at all?

MONICA

A little. I wish I had an ounce of her courage!

EVERARD

She's an unusual woman.

His even tone makes her look up at him. He looks at her with a
bright, impersonal gaze. And she sees that he loves RHODA. Her
face shows surprise, and he laughs. She puts her gloved hand on
his, delighted at her discovery.

MONICA

Are you ... May one ... ?

EVERARD

I've no idea. Miss Nunn, as you know ...

They move off, into the crowds.

MONICA

But surely there's nothing wrong. We all have a right
to happiness.

EVERARD

Absolutely!

EXT. THE ROYAL ACADEMY – DAY

They emerge from the Academy, and walk across the courtyard
together. He holds her arm and they are deep in conversation.

MONICA

I wonder. Do you remember my friend, Robert Bevis?

EVERARD

Robert Bevis? Oh yes. The young chap with the fair
hair.

MONICA

Yes. He's looking for a room to rent. I was wondering
if you might perhaps have a spare room in your
house ... ?

EVERARD

Hm ...

It is not until they are nearly at the exit that she looks up and sees
WIDDOWSON in the street, waiting in the CARRIAGE.

INT. DRAWING ROOM – WIDDOWSON HOUSE – DUSK

In the dark, dingy, over-furnished drawing room, MONICA is
sitting stiffly by the fire. WIDDOWSON is walking about, agitated.

WIDDOWSON

... and on Tuesday you were out until nine o'clock.
On Friday, when I asked you for a drive, you said
you were unwell. When I suggested taking you
to the Academy today, you implied that I knew
nothing about pictures and that my presence would
embarrass you! (*His face creases as he tries to*

control himself.) Are you ashamed of being seen with me?

MONICA

Of course not.

WIDDOWSON

Then why insist on going alone? To meet that mountebank, that's why!

MONICA

(*In a tired voice, as of an old argument*) You hate pictures.

WIDDOWSON

I was prepared to go with you.

MONICA

Yes, and grumble! You said you couldn't understand why people paid good money to put things of no use on their walls.

WIDDOWSON

That was because ...

MONICA

I can't stand it when you huff and puff behind me and want to leave all the time.

He starts to speak.

MONICA

Why shouldn't I see my friends? My friends like paintings.

He walks up and down, darting suspicious looks at her.

MONICA

I'm bound to meet people I know.

WIDDOWSON

I see. I'm good enough to provide the clothes on your
back, but not to be seen out with you ...

She flies out of the room. He hurries after her.

INT. HALL AND MORNING ROOM – DAY

WIDDOWSON follows her through the hall into the morning room,
where she has left a half-made dress and her sewing things. He
notes the untidiness with a frown.

She sits firmly, and begins to sort out her sewing.

He watches her for a long moment, then exits the room.

She winces at the sharp closing of the door.

With trembling hands, she picks up her needle and starts to sew.
She finds it hard to breathe. Her hands quiver. She fumbles for her
little scissors. She trims the edge of a seam.

WIDDOWSON enters again, and she puts down the scissors.

WIDDOWSON

I must take you away.

She looks up, her eyes showing deep dismay. WIDDOWSON paces
rapidly.

WIDDOWSON

We must leave London.

MONICA

(A little moan) No ...

WIDDOWSON

(With growing conviction) We'll find a house in the
country. (He has an idea.) Near your old home, if you
wish. Your sisters can come with us.

Having an idea stimulates him, and some of his suspicion evaporates. He turns to her, his face bright with solution.

WIDDOWSON

Well, what do you think of the idea?

She looks at him briefly.

WIDDOWSON

Isn't it worth it, to save our happiness?

She won't look at him.

WIDDOWSON

I'm trying to act for the best!

MONICA looks at him at last.

MONICA

So, I'm to be a prisoner?

WIDDOWSON

Not at all.

MONICA

You want to remove me from my friends.

WIDDOWSON

Not at all!

MONICA

You resent them.

WIDDOWSON

That is not true.

MONICA

Name one that you approve of.

WIDDOWSON

(*Caught out. Dithers.*) Ah ... Miss ... Ah, your friend
Millie?

MONICA

You haven't a good word for her.

WIDDOWSON

All I want is for us to make a fresh start.

She rises and walks to the window.

WIDDOWSON

I'm prepared to give up my home for you!

She makes a move towards the door. He blocks her way.

WIDDOWSON

I cannot allow you to roam about unchecked.

She skirts past him. He follows.

WIDDOWSON

You are my wife!

MONICA

And I can never be friends with someone who chooses
not to trust me.

WIDDOWSON

Friends? I am not your friend. I am your husband.
Your lover. Am I not your lover, the man you love?

She gives him a look of stone.

WIDDOWSON

Don't. I can't ... Don't say you've ...

He walks again, rapid, and agitated.

WIDDOWSON

You mustn't. You mustn't stop loving me.

MONICA

You might ask yourself . . .

WIDDOWSON

No. Do not say it. I am absolutely dependent upon . . .
You know very well how it is with me. I require that
you love me.

MONICA

I hate the very sound of your voice.

The hatred runs around the room. Then she turns, and walks out

He is left alone, standing in the debris of his marriage.

INT. OPERA HOUSE – NIGHT

Onstage, a scene from *The Mikado* is playing out.

ON: the stalls.

EVERARD is sitting between RHODA and MARY.

INT. FOYER – NIGHT

It's the interval.

A buzz of sound as MRS COSGROVE turns her head. HER POV:
some distance away, beyond the crush of THEATRE-GOERS, are
EVERARD and RHODA, talking. RHODA, in bright colours, looks
like a good-looking gypsy. EVERARD is talking to her with urgent
concentration.

NEW ANGLE: MRS COSGROVE is next to MARY.

MRS COSGROVE

You've kept that very dark.

MARY

Oh Christabel, you're an appalling matchmaker.

MRS COSGROVE

Why not? Someone must do something for all these spare girls. (*She cranes for another look.*)

MARY

Well, you may save your efforts. I can assure you they will be entirely wasted, on both partners.

MRS COSGROVE

(*With a shrewd look*) I should give your friend a warning, nonetheless.

MARY

(*Sharp*) What do you mean?

MRS COSGROVE

She lacks experience. Dangerous in a woman of her age.

MARY

Any age.

MRS COSGROVE

Oh, girls are green. It protects them. Different for a woman. Things get out of hand.

MARY

I shouldn't worry. My cousin is a tease. He pursues Rhoda safe in the knowledge that she is absolutely unassailable. He'll soon tire of it.

MRS COSGROVE

(*Doubtful.*) But will she?

MARY moves off, back into the auditorium.

MARY

(*Harsh tone*) Rhoda has no interest in marriage. None
at all!

MRS COSGROVE, left standing, her mouth open, watches MARY go.

ON: EVERARD and RHODA, heads together, moving out of the foyer.

EVERARD

The Lakes?

He and RHODA are separated briefly, then come together again.

EVERARD

A splendid idea. You like to climb?

RHODA

(*Nods, above someone's head.*) And then I thought
Seascale ... miles and miles of empty sand. I can run
naked into the sea.

He smiles at her – a natural, friendly smile – and follows her into
the auditorium.

EXT. COUNTRYSIDE AND HOUSE – DAY

A charming, smallish country house.

A CARRIAGE draws up. The AGENT gets out. WIDDOWSON helps
MONICA down as the AGENT holds open the gate of the house,
smiling.

He takes them up the path, pausing to point out the features of
the house.

EXT. RECTORY – DAY

WIDDOWSON and MONICA emerge from the side-door of a rather forbidding rectory.

WIDDOWSON walks on. MONICA pauses and looks up at the grim façade.

INT. EMPTY HOUSE – DAY

An ELDERLY AGENT enters the room, followed by MONICA and WIDDOWSON.

The room is light, Georgian. The views from the windows are rural and pleasant.

WIDDOWSON seems pleased with this house. He turns to MONICA for her opinion, but she gives him a wan look. She seems pale and unwell.

INT. AGENT'S OFFICE – DAY

Outside the large window is a pleasant street in a country town.

WIDDOWSON and MONICA are sitting across a desk from the agent.

WIDDOWSON and the agent talk, and lean over the table, looking at a plan of an interior.

MONICA looks trapped.

EXT. WIDDOWSON HOUSE – LONDON – DUSK

The WIDDOWSONS arrive home in a HANSOM CAB.

The ELDERLY MANSERVANT appears at the door to greet them. He takes the bag from the CABBIE, then follows WIDDOWSON into the house.

INT. ENTRANCE HALL – WIDDOWSON HOUSE – DUSK

The ELDERLY MANSERVANT takes WIDDOWSON's hat and stick.

MONICA runs up the stairs.

> WIDDOWSON
>
> Well, Harvey.

> MANSERVANT
>
> Well, sir.

> WIDDOWSON
>
> All done. We've found a house.

HARVEY is stunned.

> WIDDOWSON
>
> Own grounds. Fine views. And only a mile from the
> village. (*He is high with a sense of achievement.*)
> You're going to be very comfortable.

> HARVEY
>
> (*Doubtful.*) It'll be a big change, sir.

> WIDDOWSON
>
> I must see the agent in the morning about putting this
> house on the market. We're going to live in very good
> style.

He looks round with new disfavour at his home.

MONICA comes flying down the stairs, having changed her clothes.

> WIDDOWSON
>
> Where are you going?

> MONICA
>
> Out.

WIDDOWSON

You've just come in! Where are you going?

MONICA

To see my sisters.

WIDDOWSON

I'll drive you there. We'll go together with the good
news. I know they're praying that we've found ...

MONICA

No!

She wrests free of his hand on her arm, and runs out of the open
door, and down the path.

HARVEY looks at her in amazement – then at WIDDOWSON.

Beside himself, WIDDOWSON, snatches his hat from HARVEY, and
goes after her.

EXT. LONDON STREET – DUSK

MONICA walks rapidly towards us, her hat bobbing on her head.

At a considerable distance behind her, WIDDOWSON is hurrying
to catch her up.

MONICA crosses the road, reaching a corner, and waves wildly as
a CAB comes into view. It stops and she gets into it.

WIDDOWSON breaks into a run, waving violently at the CAB.

But it drives away.

Breathing heavily, WIDDOWSON stops in his tracks, defeated.

INT. ATTIC – EVERARD'S HOUSE – NIGHT

A small, blue-washed, angled room. A soft sound, and a gasp.

BEVIS and MONICA are clasped in each other's arms, holding on to each other for dear life. They kiss, in mutual need.

INT. VIRGINIA'S APARTMENT – DAY

In the little sitting room, VIRGINIA pours something from a small bottle into a cup of cocoa. A LOUD KNOCKING on the door.

Startled, VIRGINIA sways, then panics. She pours the cocoa down the sink, then hides the bottle in a cake-tin. MORE KNOCKING.

She runs along the passage to the door.

WIDDOWSON pushes in.

> WIDDOWSON
>
> Where is my wife?

> VIRGINIA
>
> (*Swaying*) Oh, Edmund! Such news! To think ... the country again ... little birds ... warm milk from the cow ... primroses, meadowsweet ...

He stops her from falling as she trips on the edge of the carpet.

> WIDDOWSON
>
> My wife. Where is she? Where is my wife?

VIRGINIA smiles up at him, happily.

INT. ATTIC – EVERARD'S HOUSE – DAY

MONICA and BEVIS are sitting together on a little sofa under the eaves, like two birds huddled together.

> MONICA
>
> Robert, please ...

BEVIS

If only we'd met a year ago.

MONICA

Don't make me go back to him. I'll kill myself.

BEVIS

You mustn't ...

MONICA

Take me to France with you!

BEVIS

You know I want to.

MONICA

He makes my flesh creep. He should never have made
me marry him. No, that's not fair ...

BEVIS

(*Into her hair*) Ssh!

They kiss.

MONICA

Say you love me.

BEVIS

You know I do.

MONICA

I could get a room until Tuesday.

BEVIS

Oh, darling girl. (*He groans.*) Couldn't we wait? Just
a little? I shall be arriving in a strange country. The
manager will be at the station ...

MONICA

Don't you want me?

BEVIS groans, and covers her face in kisses.

> BEVIS
>
> Yes ... oh ... yes ... yes ... yes!

He kisses her passionately. He will agree to anything. But she sees this, and the reason for it. She draws back.

> MONICA
>
> You really want me? You're sure?

He doesn't answer at once.

Her face falls as she watches him.

> BEVIS
>
> Dearest, we mustn't be rash. My mother ... my sisters
> depend on me. I'm their only support.

She groans.

A LOUD KNOCK at the door. He jumps.

> BEVIS
>
> Who's that? Ssh!

She looks at his scared face and turns away sadly as he puts his finger to his lips. ANOTHER LOUD KNOCK.

They stand, frozen. A pause, then a piece of paper is pushed under the door. Sound of steps receding.

BEVIS tiptoes across, picks up the paper, and reads it.

> BEVIS
>
> It's all right! Just a message from one of the partners
> about my journey.

His relief is total. All passion flown. He looks young and vulnerable – a scared boy. She picks up her things slowly, her head bent, and goes to the door.

                    BEVIS

Dearest?

                    MONICA

Goodbye.

                    BEVIS

But . . . the arrangements?

                    MONICA

They're not very practical, are they?

                    BEVIS

Let's wait a little while, till I'm established.

                    MONICA

(*Her hand on the door.*) You want me to go back to
him?

He comes towards her but she goes.

                    BEVIS

  Just for a . . .

He doesn't follow her.

INT. STAIRS – NIGHT

MONICA flies down the stairs. Suddenly, everything spins about
her. She sways, grasps the wall and slides down.

She sits, her head against the wall, blinking, trying to clear her
head. She tries to rise, but cannot. Eventually, she manages to get
up, and goes downstairs carefully, white and dazed.

EVERARD, coming out of his room on the first floor, is just in time
to catch MONICA as she faints.

EXT. TRAIN STATION – NIGHT

WIDDOWSON is craning and darting, trying to see everyone who passes. He walks off as a GROUP OF PEOPLE surge forward.

INT/EXT. ANOTHER PART OF THE STATION – SAME TIME

RHODA appears, walking briskly. She pauses to buy a paper. She sees an OLD WOMAN selling violets. She makes to pass by, but changes her mind. She bends, picks up a bunch, and gives the woman sixpence.

> WOMAN
> Thank you, Miss. And God bless you.

RHODA smiles to herself for being a sentimental fool. But she smells the violets briefly.

Hurrying, her attention is alerted by the SOUND OF SHOUTS.

PEOPLE are clustering around what seems to be a fight. It is in her path.

As she approaches, she sees EDMUND WIDDOWSON flailing at his wife, and being protected by EVERARD.

She watches, transfixed as EVERARD – protecting MONICA and himself – strikes WIDDOWSON. He reels back at the blow.

Something in RHODA exults.

But then EVERARD puts an arm about MONICA and leads her away, to cheers from the crowd.

WIDDOWSON picks himself up.

RHODA, the flowers in her hand, turns swiftly, walking in the other direction, so not to be seen – confusion vying with suspicion. Is EVERARD involved with MONICA?

She emerges from the station and her pace slackens.

She walks along the road, finding herself stimulated. The notion of battle with him, fills her with vitality.

Holding the flowers, she quickens her stride – her hair escaping in the breeze, a slight smile on her lips.

EXT. BEACH – DAY

RHODA is strolling along an almost deserted beach. She wears sand shoes and has her skirt tucked up, and carries a straw hat. She walks along at the water's edge, musing. She pauses to look at a shell.

She turns away from the sea, and walks up the beach. She sits. SEVERAL CHILDREN approach, followed by their NURSE, and play near her. She watches them with an alert interest.

The sound of a train. She turns her head.

The CHILDREN cry and run up the beach. The LITTLE TRAIN approaches.

RHODA rises and walks away from the children, further along the beach, and further up on the dunes, to higher ground, where convolvulus and other wild flowers grow. She stands there, looking out to sea.

The CHILDREN wave and shout as the LITTLE TRAIN chuffs by.

RHODA wanders the dune, scuffing her feet. All is still. The beach is now deserted except for a man, at a distance, coming along the shore. She turns and waits for him.

EVERARD gets closer. He waves a hand in greeting.

CUT TO:

EVERARD and RHODA walking along the beach.

RHODA

How did you know it was me?

EVERARD

(*Laughs*) I believe you're sunburned already.

RHODA

I can't think how. It's rained every day.

EVERARD

Did you bathe?

RHODA

Once. In the rain.

They walk off along the beach.

EXT. HILLS – DAY

EVERARD and RHODA are climbing in the hills, with packs on their backs. They pause to look at the awesome scenery.

He gives her his hand as they move off, but she spurns it.

They climb, passing a solitary SHEPHERD'S COTTAGE.

CUT TO:

EVERARD lies on the grass after their picnic. He looks up at her as she sits, a little above him.

EVERARD

I've imagined something like this.

She smiles at him and looks out at the view.

EVERARD

Why don't we take that cottage? (*He points to the cottage, now below them.*)

RHODA

You'd be bored in a week.

EVERARD

There's always the Bosphorous ... St Petersburg ...
The Nile?

She lies back on the grass, drawing on a cigarette, aware of him
at her feet.

CUT TO:

They are climbing again. Now, the going is tougher. He helps her
over the rock face. Then they separate, each finding the best way
up.

CUT TO:

They come together at the top of the hill, turning to each other in
triumph. She steps forward to view the scene and he watches her
profile and the movement of her hair in the wind on her face.

EXT. BEACH – DUSK

RHODA has changed into a pale dress. She looks fragile and lovely.
EVERARD embraces her. The embrace becomes more passionate.

EVERARD

I want ...

They embrace again. She draws back, in a movement suggesting
consent. Close, he bows his head before her, waiting.

RHODA

There's no-one else?

He shakes his head.

RHODA

(*Softly*) No-one at all?

EVERARD

No.

She gives him a swift, gleaming glance, but lowers her head in a decision of dismissal. He kisses her again and the embrace is prolonged and passionate. They sink down on the sand. He rolls on to her, and it seems they will consummate their love. But she drags herself up, trembling and gasping.

EVERARD

(*Mutters*) Don't you trust me?

RHODA

(*Murmurs*) Yes.

EVERARD

And you'll live with me? Give up everything?

She nods, mesmerized by the intensity of his gaze.

RHODA

What about you?

But he merely smiles, and shakes her gently, as if in triumph.

EVERARD

Good. Good.

He leans forward and kisses her gently on the lips. She lifts her arms about his neck in a slack, languid movement and they kiss once more, a mutual, loving salute, a sealing of the bargain. He lifts her left hand, kisses her fingers … and slips a ring on the third finger. RHODA draws back. She looks at her hand, then up at him, then at her hand again. She gasps, then, involuntarily, snatches off the ring and scrambles awkwardly to her feet.

EVERARD

What is it?

RHODA

Here! I don't want it. Take it!

The ring falls. He pauses to find it, and pick it up, then catches up
with her.

EVERARD

What's the matter? (*He grabs her.*)

RHODA

We should just be living a lie! Childish.

She walks on, more slowly. Again, he stops her.

EVERARD

(*Softly*) What is it? (*She will not look at him.*) Tell me
what you want. Is it marriage?

She doesn't answer.

EVERARD

We-ell!

He caresses her hair in a teasing gesture.

RHODA

Where would it get us? Just an act of defiance, it
would ...

EVERARD

(*Smiling drily*) You're absolutely right! Marriage
then.

RHODA

(*Lifts her head in panic.*) Not in a church?!

EVERARD

Very well. By licence.

He continues to look down at her lowered head. He seems pleased –
but there is a new objectivity in his glance. She looks away, along
the beach.

RHODA

(*Low*) Kiss me.

He finds the demand thrilling, and bends at once, embracing her ardently.

CUT TO: LATER

EVERARD and RHODA walk back along the sands together, a little apart. They are silent. She looks across at him more than once, a trace of anxiety in her expression. He walks purposefully. But his face is set.

A COLOURED BALL falls at EVERARD's feet. He smiles, leans forward, and pitches the ball back to a STURDY CHILD.

CUT TO: LATER

EVERARD and RHODA are on the beach, sitting against a breakwater.

RHODA

Are you hungry?

He shakes his head.

RHODA

The air's given me an appetite!

She is exuberant. He watches a BOAT out at sea, frowning against the light.

RHODA

What on earth is Mary going to say? You know what
you've done. Ruined my grand design for a dedicated
life! (*She leans forward, and kisses the top of his
head.*)

His profile, as he squints against the light, looks grimmer, and older.

EVERARD

I must go up to town ... to make arrangements. For
the ceremony.

RHODA

Oh, not in London?

EVERARD

Where then? Manchester, Stockport ... Southend?

RHODA

What's the matter?

EVERARD

Nothing. (*He covers his feeling of malaise*) I'm
impatient.

Gratified, she reaches into her bag, takes out a letter, opens it, and
begins to read. He glances at her.

RHODA

(*Waves the letter*) From Mary!

MARY (V/O)

... but I felt that you should know that Monica is
now expecting a child, and that her husband is by no
means certain that the child is his. It is very painful
for me to write this but, as your close friend, I felt it
my duty to warn you. Mr Widdowson came to me and
we spent an hour together. I managed to persuade
him against any violent course of action where
his wife was concerned and, in fact, she has been
dispatched, with her sisters, to the country, where he
has recently acquired a house. Dear Rhoda, what you
decide to do with your life must be your own decision.
But I cannot, as your friend, stand by and allow you
to contract to someone, even more to a member of my

own family, without knowing the full truth of how matters stand. Alas, this is not the first time ...

Her voice goes as RHODA drops the letter.

EVERARD

What is it?

She hands him the letter. He reads it, and hands it back to her.

RHODA

Well?

He makes no reply.

RHODA

Have you nothing to say?

He looks away, and contemplates the horizon.

EVERARD

(*Neutral*) I thought there was to be none of this.

RHODA

Tell me! The letter says your name is ... You could clear this up in an instant!

EVERARD

You feel that I am obliged to do so?

RHODA

I'm not thinking of myself, but of you.

EVERARD

I don't give a damn.

He gets up and dusts off the sand.

RHODA

Was she your mistress?

He looks out to sea.

EVERARD

It's not going to work, is it?

She looks up at him and, despite herself, tears spring to her eyes. With trembling hands, she puts the letter away, and gets up. She stands, waiting for him to come to her. But he does not move. She makes a move towards him, but finds she has walked past him. She continues to walk, very slowly. Will he come after her?

Behind her, he watches her receding figure. He makes to go after her, then, with sudden decision, changes his mind and leaps up over the dunes towards the road. He walks off swiftly in the other direction.

RHODA, in tears, goes up the wooden steps from the beach to her hotel. She stumbles, unable to see properly, grasping at the rail for support.

EXT. THE WIDDOWSON HOUSE – CLEVEDON – DAY

ALICE is weeding. She rises carefully, her back stiff, carries the trug full of weeds to a nearby pile, and walks up the flagged path to the house, humming happily to herself.

In the distance, VIRGINIA approaches in hat and coat, a basket on her arm.

EXT. RIVERSIDE – DAY

From a distance, we see WIDDOWSON standing motionless at the water's edge, under a fringe of willow. He is looking down at the water. After a long pause, he looks up, across the river, turns, and walks off along the path. His movements are stiff and strange.

He is stopped by the sight of the bridge from where he first saw Monica, sitting on a seat.

He makes a sound between a growl and a groan and turns, almost knocking over a WOMAN with a wicker pram. He retraces his steps, back along the path, now in a blind hurry.

INT. SCULLERY –WIDDOWSON HOUSE – CLEVEDON – DAY

ALICE in the scullery, washes her hands under the tap, and dries them on the roller towel. She puts her trug under the sink and walks through to the morning room.

INT. MORNING ROOM – WIDDOWSON HOUSE – DAY

MONICA is sitting in the windows seat, looking out.

> ALICE
>
> How are you, dearest?

MONICA waves a hand at the familiar enquiry. Her face is white. ALICE comes to the window and looks out as VIRGINIA walks up the path.

> ALICE
>
> Virginia's looking well. So much better.

ALICE finds her knitting, and settles down comfortably. MONICA gets up and walks restlessly. She is visibly pregnant.

> MONICA
>
> Was that the postman?

> ALICE
>
> Nothing for you dear.

They exchange a brief glance. ALICE clicks.

> ALICE
>
> (*After a pause*) Dear Edmund. He would so appreciate
> a letter.

MONICA

Why? Has he written to you?

ALICE

I know his feelings.

MONICA

That I doubt.

ALICE

A few lines – after all his generosity.

MONICA

I don't want to see him!

ALICE

Sssh. Don't upset yourself. I shall say no more. (*She picks up her knitting and does a few inept stitches.*) A few lines! He has promised not to come until you wish it.

MONICA

I don't wish it. Ever.

MONICA stands by a small table, fiddling with a china shepherdess. ALICE makes to speak, but thinks better of it. She glances at MONICA timorously.

ALICE

(*After a struggle, low*) You've deceived us, haven't you, dear?

MONICA

(*Shocked*) Why do you say that?

ALICE

You've changed.

MONICA

Changed?

ALICE

(*Tremulous*) You're not affectionate anymore. You won't see Edmund. Or allow him to ... You wait for the post every day ... (*She falters, embarrassed.*)

MONICA

I wouldn't be living here at his expense, if the child were not his.

They are both acutely embarrassed.

MONICA

It's true. I ... I haven't told you. There _was_ someone ...

ALICE

But, if it's Edmund's child, surely, he has a right to ...

MONICA

He'll never leave me alone.

ALICE

But he's given his word!

MONICA

He won't keep it. We're his! His property!

She swoops to the door.

ALICE

Where are you going?

MONICA

(*Furious, in tears.*) Out!

EXT. CHELSEA AND CHELSEA BRIDGE – DAY

RHODA is walking in Chelsea, hands in the pockets of her linen coat. The CHURCH BELLS ring for Sunday Matins.

On Chelsea Bridge, she looks at the boats, and at couples enjoying themselves. She leans to look at the swirling water.

NEW ANGLE: She walks, leaving the bridge, striding swiftly, and bumps into MRS COSGROVE, who is coming out of a CHURCH.

> MRS COSGROVE
>
> That man! Come and have a glass of sherry before I commit an offence against the parson.

She leads the way to her house cheerfully.

> MRS COSGROVE
>
> Forty minutes on the virtues of chastity with his wife in the front pew, threatening to produce number twelve before the blessing!

> RHODA
>
> (*Laughs*) A fair punishment. You shouldn't indulge in the opium of the masses.

> MRS COSGROVE
>
> (*Holding open her gate.*) Touché.

They sit in the garden. A MAID brings a tray. MRS COSGROVE pours.

> MRS COSGROVE
>
> How are you?

> RHODA
>
> In good form.

MRS COSGROVE

I hear you're working very hard. (*Glancing at her shrewdly.*)

RHODA

We shall soon need larger premises. Thank you.

She takes her glass of sherry, sips, and smiles approvingly.

MRS COSGROVE

Pity about the Widdowsons.

She looks at RHODA. But RHODA's face gives nothing away.

MRS COSGROVE

Why is one always so pleased when people smash up?

RHODA looks at her with an instant of pain.

MRS COSGROVE

It's going to have to go, you know, marriage. Children are a problem, of course – not that Edgar ever saw ours. Too busy making the means to support us all. No, we need a new arrangement. I'm even prepared to put up with the kind of humourless, boring woman who most likely will lead us to freedom.

RHODA

(*Mildly*) Christabel ... !

MRS COSGROVE

What we need is someone like you. Someone brave, bold, and beautiful.

RHODA gives her an odd, haunted glance.

MRS COSGROVE

You know you're a fine-looking woman. Much too good to go to waste.

RHODA

And what is that supposed to mean?

MRS COSGROVE

It means be sensible.

RHODA

(*Putting down her glass.*) Sometimes Christabel, I
wish you would make your mind up. Or are you only
interested in mischief?

MRS COSGROVE

Not at all. I'm merely saying that it is necessary to
choose one's path realistically.

RHODA gives her a cool look, and strides off across the grass. MRS
COSGRAVE twists her mouth, making a decision.

MRS COSGROVE

(*Calls*) Give my regards to Mary and Everard.

RHODA

(*Calls without turning.*) He's abroad.

MRS COSGROVE

(*Hurrying after her.*) No, no, my dear. Didn't Mary
tell you? He's been back a month. Mary's been helping
him to refurnish.

Standing with her hand on the gate, RHODA is turned to stone.

MRS COSGROVE comes up to her.

MRS COSGROVE

I forgot. Monica wants to see you. I think she has
something on her mind.

RHODA looks at her, a hint of tears in her eyes.

MRS COSGROVE

I had a letter. It would be a kindness.

But RHODA hurries away down the road.

INT. ENTRANCE HALL – MARY'S HOUSE – DAY

RHODA rushes into the house, slamming the door and hurling her hat across to the hall table. The study door opens and MARY appears, eyes wide at the loud slam of the door.

RHODA turns, and confronts MARY – who sees at once that she knows.

INT – OFFICE – TYPING SCHOOL – DAY

ON: EVERARD.

EVERARD

Let's not have a comedy. Will she see me or not?

MARY looks up at him. He is sitting on the corner of her desk.

MARY

It has nothing to do with me.

EVERARD

That's droll. If it weren't for that damned letter of
yours we should be married ...

MARY

I was bound to tell her!

EVERARD

But not that I was in London! I haven't called because
I presumed ... what's more, the impression I received
from you was that she had no desire to see me. You
didn't tell her!

MARY

Because she showed not the least interest in your movements.

EVERARD

You could have mentioned.

MARY

Why? What do you want? That I should plead on your behalf? Why, pray? Give me one good reason. In any case, it is none of my affair.

EVERARD

Which hasn't prevented you from intruding. Not for the first time.

MARY

So we are back to that. Well, since you choose to bring it up . . .

EVERARD

I'm not prepared to discuss it.

MARY

No. You never were.

They lock gazes.

EVERARD

Having lived under your pronounced sentence these eleven years . . .

MARY

You forget I was there at the time. That I know!

EVERARD

(*After a pause.*) That girl in Oxford was being packed off to London because she was expecting a child – no, not mine! Most likely her employer's . . . though there

were several other candidates, including our socially
benevolent host.

MARY

That I shall never believe.

EVERARD

Believe what you wish. You women live in fairyland.

MARY

If we do, it's because you put us there! (*Slight pause*)
You made her an allowance!

EVERARD

(*Drawls*) Yes. Despite your priggish lamentations. I
was sorry for her. She was in a mess.

MARY

(*After a pause.*) Why on earth didn't you say?

He looks at her angrily.

MARY

Would it have been so difficult?

EVERARD

There was nothing . . .

MARY

Oh, I think there was. I think there was, Everard.
We were, I thought at least, friends. Possibly more.
You gave me to believe it. (*She looks at him levelly.*)
Oh yes. You asked me to trust you, and I did. But you
refused to trust me. Why? Was I so inadequate . . .
unworthy? I'd fought your battles long enough. Why,
all of a sudden, was I to be ranked with the enemy?

EVERARD shrugs irritably.

MARY

Why? (*Low*) If I failed you, it was by default, not
commission.

EVERARD

If I've treated you badly . . .

MARY

I was young. I knew nothing because nothing was told
to me – least of all by you. You are exclusive, Everard.
You exclude. What are you afraid of?

He picks up his hat.

MARY

If you wish I'll speak to Rhoda.

EVERARD

Pray don't.

MARY

If I thought there was the least chance that it would
make either of you happy . . . You're conventional!
She . . .

EVERARD

Oh, stop it. Own up. You've never wanted it for her.
Have you?

He lifts her chin with his finger. She flinches, aware that he knows
of his enduring attraction for her.

MARY

Don't be less than you are.

EVERARD

I've been less in your eyes for years.

MARY

By your decision.

EVERARD

(*Slight bow*) Let's keep it that way, shall we? Fewer
disappointments on both sides. (*Smiles at her.*)
Dearest coz.

He kisses her amiably on the cheek, and goes.

MARY, behind her desk, is left utterly miserable. She rises and
goes to the window.

HER POV: EVERARD walking away – strong, masculine and
confident.

INT. DRAWING ROOM – CLEVEDON HOUSE – DAY

VIRGINIA escorts RHODA into the drawing room.

VIRGINIA

... and the housekeeper tells us that the garden is full
of bulbs. Daffodils, hyacinth, bluebell ... We can't wait
for the spring!

RHODA

You're looking well.

VIRGINIA

Yes, I'm ... Dear Rhoda, it's very good of you to come.

She embraces RHODA, then withdraws with a little smile.

VIRGINIA

I must find Monica.

She goes.

RHODA pulls off her gloves, and walks about – inspecting the room.
She turns at the sound of the door opening.

MONICA stands by the door. She is now heavy with child.

RHODA

My dear …

She goes to MONICA and kisses her.

RHODA

Are you well?

She holds MONICA at arm's length, appraises her pale face.

MONICA

(*Nods and turns her face away*) It's good of you. I do hope the journey …

RHODA

I enjoyed it immensely. Wonderful to be out of London.

MONICA indicates a chair. RHODA sits.

MONICA

I so hoped you would come. I have wanted to see you. (*Slight pause.*) It has been on my mind that I may have done you a disservice.

RHODA looks at her but does not answer.

MONICA

My … husband … made a mistake. (*She twists her handkerchief violently.*)

RHODA

A mistake?

MONICA

Yes. He saw me with Mr Barfoot, and came to the wrong conclusion.

RHODA stares at her.

MONICA

It was all a mistake!

She gets up heavily. RHODA rises to help her but is waved away.

MONICA

I had decided to leave ... Edmund ... (*She can barely say his name.*) I was taken ill. Mr Barfoot was kind enough to see me to the train.

RHODA expels her breath. Now she knows.

RHODA

(*Gently*) Could you not have explained this to Mr Widdowson?

MONICA

He would not have believed me. (*She looks away*) As it happens, he was wrong. It wasn't Mr Barfoot.

RHODA

(*Surprised*) There was someone else?

MONICA

I had to protect him! (*Pause*) Mr Barfoot and I were friends. He saw how it was. That I was unhappy. He was kind to me. He was an ally.

RHODA looks at her sharply.

MONICA

I've caused so much unhappiness! To you. To him. To Miss Barfoot ...

RHODA

To Mary?

MONICA realizes that RHODA is not aware of MARY's love for EVERARD, so she goes on quickly.

MONICA

I know what Mr Barfoot feels for you. He's never discussed it, of course. Not in so many words. But he did betray himself one day. (*She smiles.*) And I saw ... and he ... he didn't deny it. All that concerned him was that you might not ... might not return ... (*She falters.*)

Something in RHODA's face has changed – as if a light has been switched on.

MONICA

So, as you see ... It has been on my mind.

RHODA

(*Shakes herself awake.*) Don't think of it. You must think of yourself now.

MONICA

(*Absently*) Oh, there's no future for me.

RHODA

You mustn't say that.

MONICA looks at her with brave sadness. RHODA moves and sits by MONICA's side.

RHODA

We all have morbid feelings. It's your condition. But you mustn't give way. Remember, you have another human being to consider now.

MONICA

If only I had your strength.

RHODA

But you have. Of course you have! How old are you? Twenty-two? I'm thirty-two and, believe me, I don't

think of myself as old. When you're thirty, you'll look
back on all of this and smile. You've been through
a storm, yes. But there's no reason ... No reason at
all ... why you shouldn't go forward to be one of the
most contented – most fulfilled – women in England.
Trust life! Don't give in! You've a mind. That's more
than many. Be brave! Say to yourself: 'This I am
capable of, and this I will do.'

                    MONICA

I won't go back to him.

                    RHODA

Not now. Later. Make up your mind when the time is
right.

                    MONICA

Time?

She looks at RHODA with a strange expression.

EXT. HYDE PARK – DAY

A beautiful day. EVERARD and RHODA are strolling through the
park.

                    EVERARD

I'd made up my mind not to see you. Certainly not
until ... However. (*He throws a ball for MARY'S
SPANIEL*) I suppose you never would have written?

RHODA, muffled up against the cold, shakes her head with a grin.

                    EVERARD

No.

They walk.

                    RHODA

I saw Monica.

                    EVERARD

When?

                    RHODA

Last week. She's well.

RHODA picks up the ball, and throws it for the DOG.

They sit on a seat, overlooking Kensington Pond.

                    EVERARD

It was perfect, wasn't it? That day at Seascale when
we climbed the tor.

                    RHODA

(*Quietly*) Yes.

She picks up several small stones and tosses them in the water.

                    EVERARD

Do we stand as we did before?

                    RHODA

I think not. You've changed.

                    EVERARD

I'm a few months older. My feelings are just the same.

                    RHODA

But you've changed. (*She turns and looks at his face.*)
You've been travelling. You're different. I should have
to learn you all over again. Your opportunities are so
much wider than mine.

                    EVERARD

I've made a few acquaintances. Seen a few countries.

RHODA

You didn't write!

EVERARD

Neither did you.

RHODA

How can you say you love me … ?

EVERARD

It was for you to speak. You made the obstacle.

RHODA

No, that was chance. Lucky or unlucky.

EVERARD

You think it might have been lucky?

RHODA

That is hard to say.

EVERARD

(*After a pause.*) Very well. Suppose I were now to ask
you what I asked you at Seascale … ?

She throws a stone in the water. Silence.

EVERARD

Rhoda … Will you marry me?

RHODA

That isn't what you asked.

But the passion between them, which has been flickering, rises
abruptly, disturbing them both. He looks at her intently, and she
draws back, wanting to throw herself into his arms.

EVERARD

Surely the word came from you?

RHODA

Oh yes.

EVERARD

(*Takes her hand.*) What does it matter? And please forget my other suggestion. It wasn't remotely serious.

RHODA

Not serious?

EVERARD

No, of course not.

RHODA

(*Lost*) But if you weren't serious ... ? Ohh! (*She groans aloud.*)

EVERARD

What does it matter? I love you. Marry me.

RHODA

No. At least, not legally.

EVERARD

Now, <u>you're</u> not being serious.

RHODA

Oh, but I am, Everard. I spoiled everything. After that wonderful day, I lost my nerve. It still surprises me. And I apologise. I will live with you. Without marriage. As you wanted.

EVERARD

No, no. No, no, no – there's no need for that. I want to marry you. I'm asking you to marry me.

RHODA

I can't. I don't intend to marry. Ever.

EVERARD

That's impossible, you know it very well. Are you
saying that you don't love me?

RHODA

No, I'm not saying that.

EVERARD

You took that fantasy on the beach seriously?

RHODA

Didn't you?

EVERARD

Of course not. I merely needed proof of your affection.
You'd shown little enough.

RHODA

That's true.

Her coat collar turned up, hands in pockets, she thrusts out her
legs, tips her head back, and laughs.

EVERARD

What is it? Why are you laughing? I want to marry
you. Give up my freedom. Believe me, that's not
something I do lightly.

She gets up, walks on, then strikes across the grass.

She pauses under a tree and waits. EVERARD calls the DOG, who
is foraging, and catches up with her.

RHODA

No. We're strangers.

She makes to walk on, but he holds her back.

RHODA

You desire me, but you don't love me. You don't love
any woman.

EVERARD

You are quite wrong. I love women. And I love you.

RHODA

You can't.

EVERARD

Why not?

RHODA

You don't know us.

EVERARD

Marry me.

She shakes her head.

EVERARD

Why?

RHODA

If you knew me, you would know why. Please. Let's not
spoil it. It is – just – possible for us to say goodbye as
friends.

EVERARD

Why, Rhoda? Why?

RHODA

There's an ocean between us. Can't you feel it?

She looks at him sadly, and walks away. The DOG follows her. She
looks back at him once, and waves a gentle farewell.

EVERARD looks after her, his face white with disappointment and
incomprehension.

RHODA walks off, further away, the dog at her heels.

EXT. PADDINGTON STATION – DAY

WIDDOWSON, with a small travelling bag, waits for a train – his expression grim.

INT. MOVING TRAIN – DAY

WIDDOWSON on the train. He stares out of the window, unmoving.

EXT. LOCAL TRAIN STATION – NIGHT

WIDDOWSON talks to an ELDERLY PORTER, who shakes his head. WIDDOWSON begins to walk, trudging off up the hill.

EXT. CLEVEDON HOUSE – NIGHT

WIDDOWSON approaches the house and bangs down on the large door knocker. There is no sound from within.

Then the door opens and WIDDOWSON goes in.

INT. ENTRANCE HALL – CLEVEDON HOUSE – NIGHT

VIRGINIA closes the front door.

WIDDOWSON takes off his heavy coat.

                    WIDDOWSON
          Is it over?

                    VIRGINIA
          At four o'clock this morning. A little girl.

Her manner is subdued and fearful.

ALICE appears.

                    ALICE
          Dear Edmund . . .

She, too, looks fearful.

WIDDOWSON

What is it?

VIRGINIA

The doctor is with her now.

WIDDOWSON

Why?

ALICE

It was very prolonged.

WIDDOWSON

The child?

VIRGINIA

Tiny.

ALICE

Poor little thing.

VIRGINIA

She hasn't cried at all.

ALICE

Not a sound!

He feels giddy. He takes out a handkerchief, wipes his forehead.

ALICE

I was to give you this as soon as you arrived.

She gives him a bulky letter. He takes it and stuffs it in his pocket.

The DOCTOR comes down the stairs.

ALICE

Ah, here's Dr Lewis.

DR LEWIS

(*Welsh*) Mr Widdowson? I am glad to see you.

He takes WIDDOSON aside.

WIDDOWSON

How is your patient?

DR LEWIS

Unfortunately, there was a haemorrhage.

WIDDOWSON

What does that mean?

DR LEWIS

If there is a night without relapse ... (*He shrugs*)

WIDDOWSON

You mean there is a risk?

DR LEWIS

Your wife has not a very strong hold. It makes all
the difference, you see. Forgive me, I have another
patient.

He gives WIDDOWSON a piercing look, shakes his hand, and is gone.

WIDDOWSON, crossing the hall to the sisters, is stopped by the
THIN WAIL of a child above. The three of them look up.

WIDDOWSON

May I have something to eat?

INT. DINING ROOM – NIGHT

WIDDOWSON pushes his food aside, and reads her letter.

                    WIDDOWSON
     Robert Bevis!

He crushes the letter in a spasm of terrible rage.

INT. NURSERY – DAY

The next morning.

WIDDOWSON, with a face of stone, waits in the small, pretty nursery. A KNOCK. Then a NURSE enters with the CHILD. He looks down in surprise at its smallness. The NURSE puts the CHILD in his arms. He holds it awkwardly. He gazes down at the tiny child, fearful, then is overwhelmed with the desire to know if it's his child. He makes a groaning sound. The NURSE flies to his side and takes the child deftly. With a sympathetic smile, and a swift arrangement of the child's shawl, she leaves the room.

WIDDOWSON turns as the inner door opens, and an OLDER NURSE beckons him quietly.

INT. BEDROOM – DAY

MONICA lies, eyes closed, her face as white as the pillow.

WIDDOWSON is transfixed. She looks like the Sleeping Beauty.

He lurches forward, muttering. The NURSE, with a tart look, indicates he sit on the small bedroom chair at MONICA's side. He sits and the NURSE withdraws.

For a moment, WIDDOWSON can't look. Then he is drawn to the pale white face on the pillow. He gazes at her. A spasm of rage overwhelms him. But he gulps, and makes one of his strangled sounds. The chair creaks under him as he swivels away. He looks round the room, at the bowl of dried flowers, the pre-Raphaelite prints, the delicate ornaments – the pale lavender jug and basin.

MONICA's dressing-gown, soft and lacy, hangs over an elbow chair. It is the one she wore in Guernsey. He gets up, crosses, and picks up the dressing-gown. He sits, crunching it in his hands, and bends over her, more closely this time. Then he sits back, cast in rock. He can't move. He feels as if he'll sit there forever.

INT. BEDROOM – DUSK

ALICE and VIRGINIA are kneeling by the bed. The NURSE sits on one side of MONICA – WIDDOWSON on the other. His eyes never leave MONICA's face.

INT. BEDROOM – NIGHT

WIDDOWSON and the NURSE keep vigil. His eyes flicker across the bed, noticing that the NURSE is dozing. His eyes show outrage at this. But he returns to his vigil with the same, mesmerized stare.

A CLOCK strikes.

The NURSE jerks awake. Automatically, she bends to her patient. Alarmed, she checks her pulse, then she listens to MONICA's heart. WIDDOWSON watches her.

NURSE

I'm sorry, Mr Widdowson.

WIDDOWSON looks at the NURSE. The low lamplight makes his face look monstrous.

NURSE

Your wife is dead.

He seems about to fall over onto MONICA.

The NURSE moves swiftly, and helps him to his feet. He stands, rigid.

The NURSE then leans over the bed. She smooths the sheet and MONICA's hair, ready for her sisters to see her.

NURSE

There dear. All over. No more pain.

WIDDOWSON stands against the sloping wall of the bedroom, seeming to shrivel.

EXT. CLEVEDON – DAY

It is summer. The hills, lanes and meadows look their best. The Channel is blue, and the Welsh mountains look soft through the haze.

RHODA NUNN, a satchel on her back, walks through a meadow. She climbs over a stile, and up a wooded lane to the gate of a SMALL COTTAGE.

She opens the gate and walks up a path lined with flowers.

She knocks on the front door and, hearing VOICES, goes around the side of the cottage to a small orchard at the back.

EXT. COTTAGE GARDEN – DAY

ALICE and VIRGINIA are sitting under an apple tree, the baby, in a wicker pram, beside them.

VIRGINIA

Rhoda!

ALICE

We didn't expect you so early!

RHODA

I remembered the old lanes.

ALICE slops her a brimming glass of lemonade.

RHODA

Ah! I've walked from Walton St Mary.

VIRGINIA

Dearest ...

ALICE

Much too far. Come and sit down.

But RHODA approaches the pram. She looks down at the baby. The BABY, awake, looks up.

RHODA

(*Murmurs*) Well ... !

She looks down at the CHILD in wonder. VIRGINIA appears at her shoulder.

VIRGINIA

Doesn't she look well?

She continues to gaze down at the child. The SISTERS beam.

RHODA

What is her name?

VIRGINIA

Violet.

RHODA

May I pick her up? Is it allowed?

ALICE

Of course. We do it all the time. They say it's bad for them.

VIRGINIA

But she likes it!

RHODA picks up the CHILD. Her movements are tentative. She feels her lack of expertise. She looks down at the child in her arms with fascination. She touches the CHILD's small arm, and then its head.

VIRGINIA

I'll put on the peas.

CUT TO:

ALICE and RHODA are sitting under a tree. The BABY lies on a rug at their feet.

RHODA

I couldn't be more delighted.

ALICE

There's a great deal to be done.

RHODA

The old vicarage will make a perfect school.

ALICE

It will be small, of course, not more than seven or eight children to start with.

RHODA

That's very wise.

ALICE

Yes. There's been so much ... We've had such a ...
(*She rallies*). But Edmund's been most generous. It is thanks to him that we are settled.

RHODA leans over and studies the CHILD.

ALICE

And what of you? How is the institute?

RHODA

Flourishing like the green bay tree. Did I tell you
we've found larger premises?

ALICE

Oh, where?

RHODA

Victoria. And we're publishing a paper. The first issue
next month. I'll send you a copy.

ALICE

We'll subscribe! And Miss. Barfoot?

RHODA

In wonderful form. Never better. My dear, there are
changes coming. We are on the move.

ALICE

We couldn't have done it without you. The school. If
you hadn't come to Bristol to brave the magistrate.

RHODA

I hope I wasn't rude.

ALICE

You were. Splendidly. (*Smiles happily and scrambles
to her feet.*) I'll lay the table … No, stay.

ALICE walks away in her sturdy boots.

RHODA bends over the BABY again, looking for a resemblance. She
sighs. The CHILD responds.

Instinctively, she picks it up, murmuring to the CHILD, and looks
up at the trees.

The BABY becomes sleepy. She rocks her gently.

RHODA hears ALICE and VIRGINIA laugh, and turns her head.

She turns back to the BABY.

RHODA

You poor little thing. Poor creature.

The trees sigh and sway in the breeze.

RHODA

Poor little thing.

The sound of the trees becomes stronger as the screen fades.

The End.

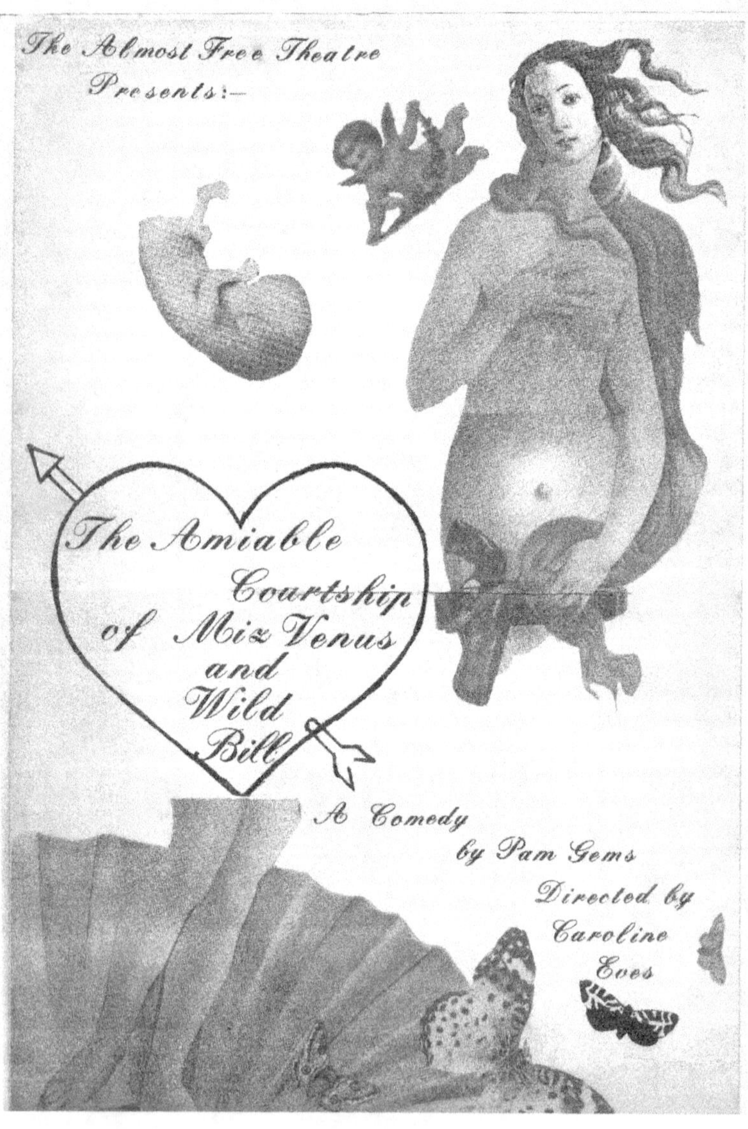

The Almost Free Theatre
Presents:—

The Amiable
Courtship
of Miz Venus
and
Wild
Bill

A Comedy
by Pam Gems
Directed by
Caroline
Eves

THE AMIABLE COURTSHIP
OF MIZ VENUS
AND WILD BILL

for Lindsay Ingram

FOREWORD

Sometime in the early seventies, I was approached by Ed Berman, artistic director of the Almost-Free Theatre in Rupert Street, W1, to write 'two sexy pieces' for his Fun-Art Bus. The idea was to tour trendy Camden, with performances on the top deck.

As a display of righteous indignation at this chauvinist request, I wrote AFTER BIRTHDAY, a monologue about a girl on remand for shoving her baby down the lav (not infrequent at mainline stations), and MY WARREN about a middle-aged office drudge sent a vibrator by vicious younger colleagues and, hating waste, using it. (If no-one loves you, there's always yourself.)

Ed took it on the chin, and put the pieces on in his theatre. Thanks to two fine, and brave, actresses, Sheila Kelley and Janet Henfrey, we were a success.

There was a hunger for plays by and about women and Ed decided to mount a season. A working group was created. We asked for women directors, administrators, and designers, and, after many readings, a group of plays was selected.

These were the days of heroic neo-feminism. It was also the baroque era of later hippie-dom – purple flares, sitar, pseudo-Marxism, and big hair. A lively time, with money for fashionable Fringe Theatre.

With 'Miz Venus,' I believe I was worried by the dismissal of the maternal in current feminist thinking. Conjugality might need a rethink, but babies still needed what babies have always needed – nourishment, protection, and love.

All the plays were well-received and, out of that season, *The Women's Theatre Group* was formed. Today, under the name *Sphinx*, it still flourishes.

Pam Gems

THE AMIABLE COURTSHIP OF MIZ VENUS AND WILD BILL was first presented by Inter-Action and The Women's Theatre Group, at the Almost-Free Theatre, 9, Rupert Street, London W.1, on the 10th of April, 1974, with the following cast:

Miz Venus	LINDSAY INGRAM
Wild Bill	DONALD SUMPTER
Myrtle	DARLENE JOHNSON
Sharon	JACQUIE COOK
Mary	JANE BRIERS
Piles	TIM STERN
Charlie	NEIL McLAUCHLAN

Directed by	CAROLINE EVES
Designed by	PATRICIA DE VILLIERS
Lighting	ROBIN HORNIBROOK
Sound	PAULINE MUTTON
Stage Manager	SURESS GALBRAITH
ASM	VALE EATON

INTER-ACTION

Artistic Director	ED BERMAN
Associate Director	PEDR JAMES
Production Manager	PETE SOUTHCOTT

THE WOMEN'S THEATRE GROUP

Production Manager	ANNE ENGEL
Crèche Coordinator	MARGARET FORD
Publicity	SHIRLEY STONE

THE AMIABLE COURTSHIP OF MIZ VENUS AND WILD BILL

CHARACTERS

MYRTLE

PROSERPINE

GLORIA

VENUS

CHARLIE

PILES

WILD BILL

RAGGED GIRL

RECEPTIONIST

RICH MAN

INDIAN MAN

INDIAN GIRL

MARY AMPLEFORTH

The play requires a cast of four women and three men.

THE AMIABLE COURTSHIP OF MIZ VENUS AND WILD BILL

<u>SCENE ONE</u>

The Stage is empty.

TWO GIRLS in fatigues enter with banners and stand at ease. The banners read 'Parthenogenesis Can Happen' and 'Your Mother Grew Your Penis.'

A THIRD GIRL enters with a soapbox, stands on it, and opens her mouth.

The Audience door is thrown open and CHARLIE, PILES and WILD BILL enter, armed.

WILD BILL jerks his head. CHARLIE and PILES drag off the THREE GIRLS.

WILD BILL upends the soapbox and sits, cuddling his weapon.

> WILD BILL
>
> Okay everybody, this is a hijack! Look, we're stronger
> than you, right? We have the hardware, right? So
> who's gonna argue?

If there is an attempt from the audience to displace him. he says:

> WILD BILL
>
> Okay, so you don't believe I'm sitting here holding
> real live ammunition that could kill you. Well, believe
> it. Suspend your imaginations. This is the way it
> happens, out there. I mean, like, this is where the
> power is at.

The lights go on the blink.

WILD BILL

Now just everybody settle down. The phones are cut
off. Okay out the back there, Charlie? Charlie, you
okay? For Chrissakes let's have some lights man!

PILES

*(Wandering on, amiable, swinging his gun. To a plant
in – or restlessness in – the audience)* Cool it. There's
live bullets in here, mush.

WILD BILL

Now listen, nobody's gonna get hurt. All we're gonna
do here is hand round some manifestos and – hey
Charlie, could I have one of them cokes and a ham
roll? Charlie?

Sound of a fracas.

GLORIA, very fat, is thrust on bearing a ham roll. She dumps it on
WILD BILL furiously.

WILD BILL

Christ. Miss Power-truck Seventy-four.

GLORIA

Watch it!

GLORIA exits with dignity.

WILD BILL

Can't avoid it. You think you're gonna find any cute
girls in this outfit? *(Calls)* You're all freaks, man! Say
Charlie, where's the coke? Charlie!

CHARLIE

(Offstage) Knock it off Bill. I got enough moody as it is.

WILD BILL

Come on, I'm dry. And send some talent this time.
How's about Venus with a coke in each hand? (*He
smirks at the audience.*)

CHARLIE

(*Off*) Coming right u-up!

WILD BILL

You kidding?

Enter VENUS, naked on a giant sea-shell, Coca-colas in each
hand, attended by THREE GRACES – MYRTLE, GLORIA, and
PROSERPINE.

WILD BILL turns, stunned, and leaps across the stage, cowering
with his gun.

WILD BILL

(*Dazed*) Wow! Thanks Charlie! (*He falls in love with
VENUS.*) Jesus Christ . . . I could definitely go for you,
baby.

VENUS

(*Strong Greek accent*) Male chovveeneest peeg.

WILD BILL

I like it. Say, where you from? You talk kinda foreign.

MYRTLE

Could we take five, Venus? Me dogs are killing me.

VENUS

(*Snarls*) You, what I rascue from account executive,
which is wanting two times a day and don' know you
on thee strit. Shot op! Whatta yor nem, beeg boy?

WILD BILL

Muh name is Wild Bill.

VENUS steps from her shell and the GIRLS robe her.

WILD BILL

Who are you? I mean, is this Märdi Gras or
something? Your phone number?

They inspect him. VENUS circles him. He is still kneeling.

WILD BILL

Hell, I know, you're the fizzy drinks queen!

VENUS looks at the GIRLS. They are not unimpressed with him.
Neither is she.

WILD BILL

Well, what's your name?

VENUS

Tekk yor cheen off my foot and maybe I tell you. (She
has a heavy, Stalinist humour.)

GLORIA

Speaking for myself, I like a bit more.

VENUS

We know. Myrtle?

MYRTLE

(Chewing gum fast and gazing at WILD BILL.) Dishy.

VENUS

Freevolous. Proserpine. (Pronounced Prosairpinny.)

PROSERPINE

(The sensible one.) There's so much to consider.

VENUS

(Squatting swiftly, like a native, looking at WILD
BILL'S feet) Yah. You are absolootely right.

WILD BILL

What the hell you doing down there?

PROSERPINE

(*Disappointed*) Flat feet?

VENUS

(*Absorbed*) I don' know. (*She touches his chaps*) What
is zis?

WILD BILL

These are muh chaps, ma'am.

She gets up, walks away, thinks, and glances at him. They lock eyes
for a moment, but she breaks it off and has a quick think. Then …

VENUS

Proserpine. Introdooce us.

PROSERPINE

Bill, you are honoured to meet – Miz Venus.

VENUS

Goddess of Love. And fertility.

WILD BILL

The hell you say!

VENUS

So, what do you theenk about that?

WILD BILL

I'd sure like to fu – marry you. I could marry you
several times right away, Miss … er …

VENUS

Venus … Venus … y'are deaf?

WILD BILL

No ma'am. I'm not deaf.

PROSERPINE

It could make a difference, you see, if you're deaf.

VENUS

I laike heem.

PROSERPINE

On the other hand, it might not.

GLORIA

You got to think about it Veen. No sense rushing. Once you get yourself hooked there's only childbirth and kkkkk *(makes a gesture of cutting throat)* to look forward to.

VENUS

Ya-as. *(She circles WILD BILL and touches his chaps)* These ... I don laike. Law of Venus. Whan you don laike, you tekk off.

She and the GIRLS laugh. WILD BILL feels a fool, but laughs.

VENUS

(Meaningfully, to WILD BILL) So!

MYRTLE

Venus, I hate to break this up but you're late for the session.

VENUS

Y'are right! *(Kisses MYRTLE fervently in thanks. Turns to audience)* Sooport thee right for women to have cortex. *(Claps a hand on MYRTLE's forehead)* As well as thalamus. *(Claps her hand on the back of MYRTLE's reeling head.)* To act as woman, not as man. To theenk as woman, not as man. To geeve suck as woman. As a woman. Forgeeve me that my Eengleesh ees so bad, bot you gat thee idea. And don' forgat. Thee geeft of Venus ees not forever. Is Pracious. Use Heem. *(She approaches the audience,)* Don' waste thee geeft of Venus. Go where you laike … where you feel true for Venus. Don' lie. Don' do for kindness, or for paying debt. Do where you want. Thees ees true. Ach … my bosoms ees full. Venus must flow!

She goes, followed by GLORIA and PROSERPINE.

MYRTLE dawdles.

WILD BILL

What was that?

MYRTLE

You hoid what she said, Mister. Miz Venus is <u>very</u> into breastfeeding. *(Gabbles, as if reading pamphlet)* Miz Venus says every woman should troy to breastfeed her choil on account of the natural colestrum in the nipples wards off infection. Likewise, kids don't throw up so much, or die from cot deaths and, if sucking natural, grow up without hang-ups – like hating their Mommy and Poppy. And Miz Venus says ladies should just take out a tit on the bus and nobody should say: 'My, ain't she common.' Likewise, guys should try not to turn around but maybe just approach the lady quietly, on alighting, with some courteous comment on the boobies, such as: that's quite a pair you have there lady, or some such formal compliment. Say, are you circumcised?

WILD BILL

(Clutching himself protectively) Why?

MYRTLE

Miz Venus says it's barbaric.

WILD BILL

More hygienic.

MYRTLE

So, wash your balls, for God's sake. But she is _not_ into vaginal deodorants. They mess up the secretions. Besides, they make it sore.

WILD BILL

(_Figuring this out, nods thoughtfully_) Uhuh. So how come you with this outfit … ah …

MYRTLE

Myrtle.

WILD BILL

… Myrtle?

MYRTLE

You wanna hear my story? You not tryin' to jump me or nothing?

WILD BILL

No Myrtle. I like your conversation.

MYRTLE exits.

WILD BILL follows her off.

WILD BILL

Honest.

ON THE SCREEN: film, or a slide, of CONTENTED COWS in meadow.

RADIO

Strontium levels in milk this year were the lowest since 61, and about 10% lower than in 68.

Contamination in calcium is now a quarter of
that recorded after the 61, 62 tests. It will now
diminish slowly as strontium enters food-stuffs from
accumulation in the soil. Fallout from recent French
and Chinese testing has yet to be recorded.

The radio rapidly changes stations and clicks off.

Fade to black.

SCENE TWO

WILD BILL enters, and looks around.

WILD BILL

Myrtle? Aw, come on, Myrtle ... look, I was only
kidding. Where are you?

VENUS appears. He turns and bumps into her.

WILD BILL

Hey ... ah ... I beg your pardon, ma'am. I was just ...
You came back.

VENUS turns to go, seemingly indifferent.

WILD BILL

Look ah ... do you need anything? Can I get you ... ?
Do you come here often?

She laughs.

WILD BILL

I'll do anything. Anything you want. Just name it.
You want me to knock off a monster, that kind of
thing? I'll do it.

VENUS

For Myrtle?

WILD BILL

You know how I feel about you. Just ask me.
Anything.

VENUS looks him up and down.

VENUS

Orright. Fatch me bottairfly.

WILD BILL

Butterfly. Butterfly? Okay. Okay, Venus. Anything
you say.

VENUS

Wait. Look for wild valerian. There you will see
tortoiseshell, peacock ... they make celebration for
Venus.

WILD BILL

I'll get 'em for you.

VENUS

One. Only one. Thee silvair fritillary with a tattered
wing. Bring hair to me.

She lets him kiss her on the arm and goes.

WILD BILL

(*Feeling foolish*) Jeez! Ah, what the hell. Crazy broad!
Who does she think she's come as? She's a kook.
Goddess!

There is a ROLL OF THUNDER, ominous.

CHARLIE and PILES enter with PLACARDS.

PILES

Stormy weather.

WILD BILL

Where the hell have you two been? And why the fuck
are those in Chinese? Don't answer, anyway, what do
they mean?

PILES

Well, this one reads 'Best of Luck, Lorraine, from all
at 43.'

WILD BILL clouts him.

PILES

Hey, cut it out!

WILD BILL

Okay, so what do you know about butterflies,
smartass?

PILES

(*Eager*) Butterflies? Oh, you're on my subject there,
Bill.

CHARLIE

(*Cuts in*) For Christ's sake, you two! We've gotta
problem backstage!

PILES

Oh yeah!

WILD BILL

What's the matter?

CHARLIE

Guy on the lights, innit?

PILES

Yeah. Been turned into a Cyclops.

CHARLIE

A centaur.

WILD BILL

Make your mind up. Which is it?

WILD BILL exits.

PILES and CHARLIE wait. There's a LOUD NEIGH.

WILD BILL

(Off) Holy smoke!

PILES

Charlie?

CHARLIE

Yup?

PILES

Did you notice anything funny about that Cyclops?

CHARLIE

I never got too close.

PIES

He was cross-eyed.

CHARLIE

Aw, come on.

They pick up their banners and slouch off, as if for guard duty.

Light change.

<u>SCENE THREE</u>

WILD BILL enters, dressed for heavy travel.

Wind noises. Back projection shots of jagged, foreboding mountains.

WILD BILL trudges, then bivouacs. He wraps himself in his blanket and curls up to sleep.

He is jerked awake by a GIRL standing over him, carrying a furled flag.

WILD BILL

Whassamatter?

MARY

I say, do you mind if I join you?

WILD BILL

(*Sleepy*) Sure.

MARY

I'm Mary Ampleforth.

She sticks out a hand and he grasps it limply.

MARY

Where are <u>you</u> bound for?

WILD BILL

Over the mountains – cross the desert.

MARY

Oh, tough cheese.

WILD BILL

What about you? Where you headed?

MARY

Oh, I've just left.

WILD BILL

What do you mean, left?

MARY

I walked out.

WILD BILL

Oh.

MARY

To be absolutely frank, I don't know why it took me so
long!

WILD BILL

Did you have a fight?

MARY

Do you know ... I say, what's your name?

WILD BILL

Bill.

MARY

Do you know Bill, it came to me in an absolute
moment of truth! My whole life, trying to please other
people. I reassure – therefore I am!

WILD BILL

Huh?

MARY

Whenever anything goes wrong, who feels guilty?
Earthquake in Tokyo. Floods. Pay dispute. You name
it. Ever since I was a kid! Had to go to bed at seven in
order to pray for everybody. And, as for boys ... !

WILD BILL

(*Perking up*) Uhuh?

MARY

Disaster! Spots, bifocals, inferiority complexes . . .
You name them, I home in on them. I'm a rest-home
for anxious penises. Do you know Bill, if you were to
make a pass at me this minute – drawers round the
ankles before you could say Danish pastry, to save
you from rejection syndrome. Frightful, you must
agree.

WILD BILL

So, you mean, you don't put out any more?

MARY

Oh, no, I didn't actually say that.

WILD BILL

That's great. What I mean is: I've been up here for five
days and my Meta tablets are just about all through,
and I could use a little warmth and company, I'm
tellin' ya! (*Flips open his blanket*) Come on in.

MARY

(*Joining him promptly*) Oh thanks. Obviously, you
don't suffer from gender angst. Of course, I realise
that, up here, even the Phantom of the Opera would be
a welcome guest.

WILD BILL

You're a very nice-looking girl.

MARY

Really? Do you mean that? (*She suddenly jumps
up*) He's looking at my legs. Objective sex, it's all
happening again. Be Firm, Mary! (*She grabs the*

furled flag.) You've got to understand. All my life it's
been evening classes and other people's children.
(She unfurls her beautiful blue silk flag.)

> WILD BILL

That's nice.

> MARY

This is for me – Mary! Bill, from the moment I walked
away from that office, <u>without</u> putting the cover on
my typewriter … all the way to the coach station,
each step away from mother, I said to myself …
Mary … Mary, from now on, YOU'RE ON YOUR
OWN … you're on your own, and it's going to be YOUR
WAY! *(She whirls and stands astride him.)* So, you
just climb out of that blanket before I tear it off you!
(She engulfs him.) Could you try and look a bit more
like Humphrey Bogart?

> WILD BILL

Well I …

> MARY

You could try saying 'play it again Sam,' or 'drop the
gun, Louie' …

She bounces up and down on him, humming *'As Time Goes By.'*

> WILD BILL

Play it again, Sam. Drop the gun, Louie. Play it again
Sam. Drop the gun Louie. Play it again Louie. Drop
the gun Sam …

> MARY

Humphrey, Humphrey …

VENUS enters, dangling a HEAD OF HUMPHREY BOGART over
MARY who grasps it in ecstasy.

MARY

Humphrey! Where is your body?

MARY suddenly realizes it is VENUS, and flees.

VENUS

You! Fethless! I stroke you daid!

WILD BILL

Venus, the word is strike. Stroke is in the past tense.

VENUS

I pastense you!

WILD BILL

– or else it means an elongated caress.

VENUS

I kress you!

LIGHTNING flashes.

VENUS

Fethless!

WILD BILL

Princess, you're gonna turn me right off, I'm telling
you. Okay, you can knock me out. Pow! Where's it
gonna get you? In the end, you're gonna have to be
nice to me. You want me to get a stand for you, you
gotta treat me nice.

VENUS

(Being nice to him) You mean laik thees? How you
like that, little tramp, hanh?

WILD BILL

I was working up to you.

She bites him, swift and venomous.

                    WILD BILL
Ow! Look, I was just getting rid of balls-ache.

She threatens him. He comes clean.

                    WILD BILL
I liked her.

                     VENUS
Is bettair. You spik truth on my sister. Go now.

                    WILD BILL
Where?

                     VENUS
Into thee desairt.

She goes, to LOUD MUSIC.

                                        Fade to black.

SCENE FOUR

The MUSIC moderates swiftly to Big-Country Western.

WILD BILL, pack on back, tackles the desert. It gets to him and he
is reduced to crawling exhaustion.

                     RADIO
For the man who has everything. Why not surprise
him with our World War 2 chess set? Complete in
white gold – uniforms hand-sewn in southern slope
alpaca – shade-side animals lack that tiny bit of lustre
and we wouldn't touch them. Chess table in chequered
marble from the quarry neighbouring Henry
Moore's in downtown Carrara. A truly deductible art
treasure. Hurry now while stocks last.

During this speech, a MAN IN RESORT CLOTHES enters with a portable bar and stool in one. He sits, drinking a highball.

WILD BILL crawls in and lifts an exhausted hand, which the MAN swats absently away.

                    MAN
You think it's fu-un being the man who has
everything? (*He drinks.*) Uh-uh. Every Christmas,
problems! We have everything … and (*darkly*) I mean
everything. Tough. You know Flamora really knocks
herself out. I wish some of our friends had her talent
for picking the right home gift. Last year, we got a
trampoline. Everybody knows I have a bad back. And
a year's lessons in limbo dancing. We got an electric
garage-door opener that spooked every jailhouse
gate from here to Fort Worth, and a Great Dane that
can bark 'Oh Canada.' But how can you quit? Without
luxury goods, the whole damn kit and caboodle
goes on the slide. Stop spending and where are you?
There's such a thing as civic responsibility, I'm telling
you. Could end up having people staying at home
sewing and baking, like the bad old days. Sweating
around in the fields instead of using their hand
massagers and watching TV. It's a sobering thought,
I'm telling you.

                    WILD BILL
Water, water.

                    MAN
Sorry Buddy, it's not a growth stock. Hi, Spiro!

He lurches off, a dignified drunk.

WILD BILL rests.

RADIO

Locusts have terrorized farmers since the beginning
of recorded history. Even recently there have been
five plagues in Arabia, Africa and Asia, and research
is now exploring the habits of schistocera gregaria,
as the locust is known, hoping to forecast when the
locust will change from his green and benevolent
phase to the black and gregarious phase ... then it
becomes necessary to strike.

Enter HINDU MAN and GIRL.

HINDU GIRL

Question. What can be manufactured for three
pounds and powered by four pennyworth of cow
dung?

HINDU MAN

A radio. Question. What could provide technical
schools for the whole of Africa?

HINDU GIRL

The cost of developing the Ford Maverick car.
Question. What to do with person who designs and
makes an electronic tie-selector?

HINDU MAN

Answer. Let him eat his own dung and drink his own
piss.

They go.

Light change.

SCENE FIVE

WILD BILL staggers to his feet and reels. The THREE GRACES enter.

                    GLORIA
He'll never make it.

                    WILD BILL
Gimmee a break, will you?

They give him food and water.

                    MYRTLE
Why don't you quit, Bill, while you still can?

                    PROSERPINE
We'll show you the way back.

                    WILD BILL
I have to get to this valley.

                    PROSERPINE
Oh Bill . . . even if you make it, you'll never find the
silver fritillary.

                    GLORIA
You better come wiv us while you're still alive.

                    MYRTLE
Before the coyotes get you, like they did the last one.

                    PROSERPINE
Give up, Bill!

                    MYRTLE
While you can.

                    WILD BILL
I've been thinking about it.

GLORIA

You've got yourself to consider.

PROSERPINE

Do what YOU want, Wild Bill.

WILD BILL

Yeah, you're right. (*Gets up*) Okay. You girls gonna
show me the way out of here?

GLORIA

Our pleasure.

MYRTLE

Where would you like to go?

WILD BILL

I need to find a fucking butterfly, so's I can get into
this wacky, bad-tempered Greek chick. And don't ask
me why I want to do that because I don't know!

They shrug and lead the way off.

Fade to black.

SCENE SIX

CHARLIE and PILES are playing draughts (checkers).

CHARLIE

You're huffed. (*Takes PILES's pieces from board.*)

PILES

Hey, what are you doing? What you mean – huffed?

CHARLIE

I take your pieces. You could have taken me and you
didn't, therefore you're huffed.

PILES

You fascist capitalist bastard. I don't have to take you
if I don't want to.

CHARLIE

If you can, you have to.

PILES

Bollocks.

CHARLIE hands him a large SWEAR BOX. He pays up with bad
grace.

PILES

But I'm not huffed. Look, I took everything else. How
could I take those, when I was taking those and those
and those and those?

CHARLIE

I didn't make the rules, Piles.

PILES

Bollocks. *(Money into swear box.)* Anyway, where's
Wild Bill got to?

CHARLIE

Trying to find some hay for the Cyclops.

PILES

He's got a real eye for the ladies, that Cyclops.

CHARLIE

Sure as hell doesn't have two.

PILES

Crown me. (*He has outflanked CHARLIE on the board.*)

CHARLIE

Piles would you mind keeping your mind on the game? I'm trying to teach you.

They concentrate.

CHARLIE

Could you stop clicking your fingers? Makes it hard to concentrate.

PILES

Sorry.

CHARLIE makes his move, after a false start. PILES pounces at once and clears the board.

CHARLIE

Fuck! (*Into the swear box.*) Well where the hell's Wild Bill?

CHARLIE rolls a joint moodily. They share a smoke during the next sequence.

PILES

Probably feeling up the Greek lady. (*Winces skywards in case she hears him.*)

CHARLIE

Yeah, trust him to get knacked by a real ballbuster. It makes your piles bleed – oh, sorry.

PILES

S'all right.

CHARLIE

You think it's gonna be so fucking great ...

PILES puts the swear box under his nose, but he doesn't notice it.

CHARLIE

... once you get out of fucking school. You think it's
going to be a real trip through the forest.

PILES

Eh?

CHARLIE

There she'll be, crying her little eyes out.

PILES

Who?

CHARLIE

Snow-white!

PILES

Yeah, seven dwarfs. Some groupie!

CHARLIE

Watch your mouth, Piles. I seen that film 41 times.
Someday, I'm gonna meet a girl like that. Long dark
hair, skin like milk, little squeaky voice. Blue birds
flying all round our heads.

PILES

It's just the joint talking, Charlie.

Light change.

SCENE SEVEN

Enter the THREE GRACES, in fatigues.

They overcome THE BOYS who put up a pitiful fight with a lot of swearing. THE GIRLS pick up LARGE BASKETS.

> CHARLIE
>
> (Disarmed) What's going on?

> GLORIA
>
> Hijack.

> CHARLIE
>
> Don't be stupid. We was here first!

> PILES
>
> No kidding.

GLORIA looks around, and kicks away their unattended guns.

> GLORIA
>
> So, what's your outfit, Painless?

> CHARLIE
>
> We're here on a peaceful mission.

> PILES
>
> Just putting our side that's all. We wanna be liberated and all.

> CHARLIE
>
> What are you girls into?

> MYRTLE
>
> Feeders United.

A SLIDE SHOW is projected on the screen, showing an image of TORTILLA AND BEANS.

GLORIA and MYRTLE hand out TORTILLA AND BEANS to some
of the audience.

MYRTLE

Breakfast in South America … tortilla and beans.

GLORIA

Dinner in South America … tortilla and beans.

PROSERPINE

With occasional salt fish. (*She crosses to the screen,
and indicates slides with a pointer.*) The manna of
the Bible is composed of the excretions of the aphis …
the shit of the greenfly that drinks the dew on the
tamarisks of the Negev and the Sinai.

GLORIA

The excretion dries like snowflakes and drifts over
the desert … mmmm.

MYRTLE

What we have to do is increase the desert dew by
planting spiny shrub and thistle …

PROSERPINE

Which will increase the transpiration giving still
more moisture …

GLORIA

Small crops … peas and beans …

PROSERPINE

Salads and tubers …

GLORIA

Melons!

MYRTLE

Cucumbers, citrus trees …

GLORIA

Grapes!

PROSERPINE

The moisture of the world is not finite.

ALL

The moisture of the world is not finite.

MYRTLE

Wet the lips.

GLORIA

We live by secretions.

PROSERPINE

And by effort.

They pick up the baskets.

GLORIA

(*To PILES*) So you wanna be liberated?

PILES

Yeah. I think so.

THE GIRLS confer.

GLORIA

(*To PILES*) Here, Eggcup, I got a proposition for you.

PROSERPINE

(*To CHARLIE*) You see Charlie, let me put it this way.
We're in the construction business.

CHARLIE

(*Interested*) Oh yeah?

MYRTLE

Terrific prospects Chuck ... you really get to climb.

They persuade THE BOYS off.

CHARLIE

(*Going*) Climb? You mean it?

PILES

It's not anyfink to do wiv work is it? Only I'm on
doctor's orders not to work. I can do anyfink else –
just so long as it's not work.

Light change.

SCENE EIGHT

The screen shows foothills then awesome mountains … canyons,
glaciers, sheer faces, and snowy peaks.

WILD BILL enters. He looks toughened. He is tired.

WILD BILL

Tough pass,
long trail, like iron.
Yet with strong steps
we climbed that peak:
green mountains like oceans,
setting sun like blood.

Now we can pick up the moon
in the generous sky,
and catch turtles in all five oceans.
Triumphant return with talk and laughter:
Nothing difficult in the world
if you can keep climbing.

He sits. A GIRL enters.

>   GIRL
>
> Please sir …

He gets up, takes her bundle.

>   WILD BILL
>
> Sit down by the fire. Are you hungry?

He gives her food and she falls on it. He watches. She looks up and
is ashamed.

>   WILD BILL
>
> You live up here?

She nods.

>   WILD BILL
>
> It's beautiful.

>   GIRL
>
> The land is poor.

>   WILD BILL
>
> Plenty of rainfall. Good phosphates.

>   GIRL
>
> It all gets washed down there.

>   WILD BILL
>
> Then live down there.

>   GIRL
>
> We're mountain people.

>   WILD BILL
>
> Build a dam.

>   GIRL
>
> Will you help us?

He looks at her, tired, but gets his things together.

The screen shows a DAM IN CONSTRUCTION.

Complete, it is majestic in the sun.

MUSIC and SMALL BELLS sound (live).

> GIRL
> A bridge flies from north to south, natural barrier
> turned into an open road.
> High in the gorges a rock dam rises, cutting off the
> mountain's cloud and rain.
> Now is the time
> For heroes.

She goes.

> *Light change.*

SCENE NINE.

THE THREE GRACES enter with CHARLIE, PILES and WILD BILL.
They flop down.

> GLORIA
> If Bill hadn't ov took them corners so swift, the gas
> would've lasted till we could of free-wheeled. He don't
> think.

> CHARLIE
> Lay off love, we're on the way down, ain't we?

> PROSERPINE
> Every time I doze off, I'm still lifting rocks.

> PILES
> You can say that again.

PROSERPINE

Every time I . . .

PILES throws his hat at her.

WILD BILL

(Apart, resting, his hat tipped over his eyes.)
This side, other side,
only white wilderness.
Mountains, silver snakes dancing:
plateaux, white elephants running,
rivers and mountains so beautiful
heroes compete
in bowing humbly before them.
Pity the Emperors,
not enough talent.

CHARLIE

Never mind talent, I'd settle for a pair of boots.

PROSERPINE

I think I'll make myself a dress. Something soft. Silk
chiffon. Cream, no, pale yellow, with bell sleeves and
ribbon under the bust. Oh, just think of it . . . clean
undies! I'll make some new knickers in white satin
with yellow roses . . .

MYRTLE

All I need's a bath. Jeez . . . think of it . . . orange peel
shampoo, conditioner, setting lotion . . . Soak these
(Her hands) in almond oil. Get all the muck off. Dash
of talc, splash of cologne – well, you feel a new doll!

GLORIA

I can't make up me mind wevver to start wiv proan
cocktail or melon. (Sighs heavily.) Yeah . . . half a

charenty, then seafood wiv Hellman's and salad.
Porterhouse, mushrooms, french beans and grilled
tomatoes … touch of the old caramel oranges wiv
gingah – sip of me Dad's brandy. An After-Eight and
a bloody great mug of Blue Mountain coffee. How that
do you?

CHARLIE

Shut up love.

PROSERPINE

What are you going to do when we get down, Piles?

PILES

I'm having a zoo, ain't I?

MYRTLE

What for?

PILES

Oh, not _for_ nothing. You don't have a zoo _for_ nothing.

CHARLIE

Bleedin' hard work, mate. Think of all the turds. All
shapes and sizes.

GLORIA

Yeah, every new moon another Taj Mahal.

PILES

I shall use it as fuel.

MYRTLE

All worked out, eh Piles?

PILES

I've made a list of what I want. You know, to start wiv.
Very hard picking birds.

MYRTLE

(*Innocent*) Is it Piles?

PILES

(*Oblivious*) I like 'em all, see.? Tanagers, painted
quail, sandpipers, yellow hammers. As for the
waders ...

CHARLIE

We'll take your word for it me old son. Come on, gotta
make base camp. (*Gets up, freezes.*) Listen.

They all listen.

GLORIA

I can't hear nothing.

PROSERPINE

You used to hear the water rushing down the gorges.

CHARLIE

What I meant. Not anymore. (*They grin.*) Come on
Bill.

Light change.

SCENE TEN

WILD BILL moves. He sees something. There is a swirling effect in
the warm light, as of a swarm of butterflies.

Very slowly WILD BILL tips his hat forward until it falls on his arm.

WILD BILL

(*Soft*) Got it.

GLORIA

What is it Bill?

WILD BILL

Caught me a butterfly. Say Piles, you wanna take a look?

PILES

Yeah. Yeah! That's beautiful, Bill.

WILD BILL

What's it called?

PILES

It's a butterfly, innit?

WILD BILL

I know that Piles. What kinda butterfly?

PILES

Pity it's not a better specimen. Look, the wing's all ragged.

WILD BILL

What's it called, Piles?

PILES

Eh, you've got a rare one Bill. Oh, you see plenty of admirals, speckleds, painted ladies up here. Not many of those.

WILD BILL

(Trying not to hit him) What Piles? Many of what?

PILES

That . . . is a silver fritillary.

WILD BILL whoops for joy, the butterfly between his hands.

> PILES

First time I've seen a live one, you want to hang on to it, Bill.

> WILD BILL

You betcha life.

He pores over his cupped hands. Then

> WILD BILL

Oh hell! (*He lifts his hands and lets it go.*) Now why in frigging hell did I want to do that?

> *Fade to black.*

SCENE ELEVEN

A RAGGED GIRL enters.

The THREE GRACES rerobe her. It is VENUS.

VENUS and WILD BILL sit together. He kisses her gently.

> WILD BILL

I let the butterfly go.

> VENUS

Is oll right . . . is me the bottairfly. Look, one bruise you geeve me.

> WILD BILL

What do you know?

> VENUS

So? (*Smiling, then*) What's thee mattair, you change your mind?

WILD BILL

(*Taking hor hand*) No. But I did a lot of thinking out
there on the mountain. You're sure one hell of a lovely
lady and it would be a privilege to ball you <u>any</u> day
of the week. But then I got to reasoning. Shit, a man
needs … what I mean is, what I'm saying is … I don't
want no one night stand with you. Not with you. Not
with my goddess.

VENUS

So?

WILD BILL

I've done a lot of travelling for you, Venus.

VENUS

Yais.

WILD BILL

Couldn't we have a more permanent arrangement?

She looks him over slowly. It unnerves him.

WILD BILL

Jesus Christ, I'm asking you to marry me, baby! I'm
willing to give up muh freedom, I can't say fairer
than that! Now what do you say?

VENUS

(*After a long pause*) I don' know.

He lifts his head in soundless irritation.

VENUS

Maybe.

His eyes light.

VENUS

Maybe no.

WILD BILL clicks his fingers to CHARLIE and PILES, who exit.

VENUS

Possible.

WILD BILL

That's great! There's just one thing . . .

VENUS

You min yor offehr ess condeetional?

WILD BILL

Kinda.

VENUS jerks her head for her GIRLS to go. They disappear.

VENUS

You make bargain, with Venus, Goddess of Love and
Fertility!? You dare to approach prasance of Venus
with . . .

WILD BILL

But this is just what I'm trying to tell you! Quit being
such a goddamed loudmouth! Listen, when a guy's on
the loose, he's Kirk Douglas, Okay? He wants a broad.
If she runs from him, or at him, it really don't make
too much difference. He's on the loose – there's just
the one idea. But this is different! I'm sitting here
saying I want to shack up with you, permanent. But
for Christ's crying out loud, how in hell do you expect
me to get a stand for you for the rest of my natural
life, when you keep busting my balls?

VENUS

(Snarls) You –!

They grapple.

WILD BILL

Now you keep still and listen. I want a woman who'll
be pleasant, who'll respect my son and love my
daughter ... little girls suck tit too you know ... and
sometimes, sometimes it's pretty damn hard to be a
man. You ever think of that? If all you want from me
is ...

VENUS

(Breaking away from him, smoothing herself, mildly)
Have you feeneeshed?

WILD BILL

(Roars) No!! No. What I'm saying is you can't shout
around the place, making the play all the time,
because no guy worth the having is gonna stand up
with you unless you can make him half believe he's
something.

VENUS

You theenk I am too forward, Bill? (She is nice to
him.)

WILD BILL

That's better. That's much better.

They start to make love.

Light change.

SCENE TWELVE

VENUS

(Murmurs) Of course you are cot?

                    WILD BILL
What?

                    VENUS
You are cot ... cot? I don' go weeth no man who ees not
cot.

                    WILD BILL
What do you mean?

                    VENUS
You don' have vasectomy?

                    WILD BILL
The hell I don't!

                    VENUS
What you min? You theenk Venus ees on thee Peel ...
? You want I am Pragnent?

                    WILD BILL
What's wrong with that?

                    VENUS
You theenk I am making baby with mere mortal
anyboddies? You want me to be Norsemaeed?
Housewife?! Destroction on arrogant mortal! You
are looking at Career Woman. To have appointment
wiz me, you moss wett six wikks! I am Top of my
profession!

She clicks her fingers.

PILES enters in a surgeon's outfit.

                    VENUS
Tekk heem away ... and do eet quick. I feel my ardor
born inside me.

                    WILD BILL
Over my dead body!

                    VENUS
Eet will be!

                    PILES
Come on Bill. She'll turn us into choc ices!

                                        Fade to black.

SCENE THIRTEEN

GIRL at reception desk.

WILD BILL enters in dark blue suit, hair slicked down.

                    WILD BILL
(Clears throat) Excuse me, my name's *(Clears throat.)*
Ahem, Wild Bill. I have an appointment with Miz
Venus at the Fun Centre.

                    GIRL
Of course, welcome! This way. Oh, and may I offer
congratulations, sir. It's been such a popular choice
with us girls at the plant. *(Lowers voice)* I hear the
little op was no trouble. Gloria, my sister, tells me the
surgeon was a personal friend. Well that's so nice.
Believe me, you'll be so much more comfortable.

                    WILD BILL
I ... ah ... I hear it's reversible.

                    GIRL
(Darkly) I wouldn't count on that. Here we are!
Funtime!

She rings a silly bell and goes.

On the screen: slides of a CARNIVAL. ROLLERCOASTERS, RUDOLPH VALENTINO, DOLPHINS, PINTABLES – whatyouwill.

THE GRACES enter with cushions, fans, and bowls of grapes.

Enter CHARLIE and PILES in kaftans and turbans. Hubblebubble.

> CHARLIE

Hey, it's Bill! How's it coming, Wild Bill?

> WILD BILL

Great.

> GLORIA

You're looking ever so clean and tidy, Wild Bill.

> MYRTLE

Is that how she likes you?

> CHARLIE

Not the same though. I mean, it can't be, can it?

> WILD BILL

What do you mean?

> PROSERPINE

Does it leave a scar?

> MYRTLE

Come on, let's have a look.

> WILD BILL

Cut it out.

> CHARLIE

Ooh, steady on, Bill.

> GLORIA

Well I wouldn't like it.

She and MYRTLE whisper and giggle.

PROSERPINE

Our cat got ever so fat after it.

MYRTLE

(*Breaking away from GLORIA*) Wouldn't make no
difference to me.

CHARLIE

Thassit Myrt, keep it coming.

PILES

When's the orgy going to start?

CHARLIE

Yeah, let's forget old Bill's goolies.

PILES

(*Sees ice-cream on tray. Breaks away from GIRLS*)
Oooh, me favourite! Rhubarb sundae!

PROSERPINE

(*Offers WILD BILL a drink*) Are you allowed to drink
now, Bill?

WILD BILL takes a drink and stands apart.

WILD BILL

Genghis Khan,

only knew how to pull the bow,

shooting eagles.

Pity the Emperors,

not enough talent.

PROSERPINE

What was that Bill?

GLORIA

I bet Venus is making herself real fancy.

VENUS enters wearing a modestly cut blue crepe dress with a white collar, small white hat and gloves ... Jeanne Craine style.

She carries a small posy.

WILD BILL

Hey!

VENUS

Sorprise? I got your flowers.

They sit and she inspects him.

VENUS

I like.

WILD BILL

(*Looking at her*) Yeah.

The OTHERS leave informally.

PROSERPINE brings them tea, formally. They sip decorously.

VENUS

Forgive me mention but – the opairation?

WILD BILL

Yup.

VENUS

So conseederate. You onnerstand my situation Bill, hanh?

WILD BILL

Sure, sure. Anything for you, lovely lady.

He starts to move in on her.

> VENUS

Bot Beel . .

> WILD BILL

What is it?

> VENUS

Yar ollso lohving me for myself? Ees not just Sax you
are wanting weeth me?

> WILD BILL

Hell, I want to marry you, don't I?

> VENUS

Good. You got thee passports?

He pats his breast pocket.

> VENUS

We go for honeymoon now, hanh?

She nestles up to him as he picks up an AIRPORT BAG and cameras
on straps.

They go.

On the screen: Scenes of natural and man-made wonder. Some of
the places and shots are a bit unexpected.

LOUD ECSTATIC MUSIC dying to a melodious tremolo – which is cut
by a PIERCING YELL from Venus.

> *Light change.*

SCENE FOURTEEN

VENUS appears, in flat shoes and a smock, very pregnant.

                    VENUS

Where ees he? Breeng heem to me! He shall be
chained to rock of fire for thousand yeas! I weel peek
out hees eyeballs weeth thorn, and crosh hees lags
weeth chariot of steel! Breeng heem . . .
. . . aaahhh!!

Clutches her belly.

THE GRACES enter and support her.

She groans melodiously between thoroughly anal grunts.

Sound of BABY crying.

THE GIRLS shove a quick bedhead behind VENUS and arrange her
for visitors.

                    VENUS

(Cooing over BABY) Octually he's rather swit. Soch
rude leetle man, don grab so hard, oh . . . oh I lak
heem. Dorty boy, nappy ees oll dorty, that's good
hanh? Soch beeg haid, soch trobble for me. Oh, this
fidding mekk me tired. Rilly I fill quite fent oll thee
time. Thee strangth running out of my arms. Where
ees Beel? Beel, where is vitamin and fatch grepp. I
moss have grepp. Dr Yatta recommend.

WILD BILL enters with soft toys, a football, and forms.

                    VENUS

(With pleased squawk) What you got . . . oh!

Hoarse cries of pleasure. She kisses him and BABY passionately.

                    VENUS

What for oll these peppairs?

WILD BILL

We have to register the baby. Give him a name.

VENUS

A name! He shall be called Pierre Tatu ... stone and
river, rock and water. Truly I would laike many
cheeldren. Pipple thee world. But I have, already,
many children. (*Lifts BABY*) We moss celebrate –
what we have!

She holds the BABY high.

MYRTLE taps her on the shoulder and whispers, consulting a
daybook. VENUS nods – gives the BABY to WILD BILL – and is
helped into a white overall.

MYRTLE

Mr Greenboig's waiting Venus. You know how noivous
he gets.

GLORIA

Is that the feller eats candy in the waiting room?

PROSERPINE

He's a disgrace to oral hygiene.

VENUS

Right. We see to heem, hanh? (*Her Stalin smile.
Turns to audience*) Dohn't worry. Dohn't worry.
Because I now come among you in my career of lady
danteest. I don't breaking my spell. I am still ollways
lohving weeth you. I don't desairting. Is ollways steel
love. But when you come to our ladies' clinic here,
for axcallant work on yoor tith, you are babysitting
for us when you wait yor turn, no? This way we
are sharing, and no ladies sitting at home with

despairings. And no cheeldrens shut up in little cages and things.

She grasps the CHILD roughly and kisses him.

                    VENUS
What a lovely beeg boy.

She embraces WILD BILL as well.

                    VENUS
But is time for dreeling now!

PILES, with camera, puts up a hand to delay her.

Graciously she poses, with ENTOURAGE, for a formal photograph.

                                        Fade to black.

The End.

DARLING BOY

by Pam Gems from the novel
'Chéri' by Colette

DARLING BOY

The play takes place in Paris in the private apartments of the hotel belonging to Cléa de Lonval, and in the grounds and conservatory of L'Hotel Peloux, owned by Cléa's contemporary, Charlotte Peloux. The time, the Twenties.

CHARACTERS

CLÉA DE LONVAL – a stylish woman, 49 years of age.

DARLING BOY – Frédéric Peloux, her godson and lover, 23.

ROSE – Cléa's maid.

MASSEAU – Cléa's friend and ex-lover, 57.

CHARLOTTE PELOUX – Frédéric's mother, a coeval of Cléa's.

EDMÉE – young and comely, 18.

DARLING BOY

ACT ONE

ACT ONE – SCENE ONE

A salon on the private floor of CLÉA DE LONVAL'S hotel in Paris.

Time: the Twenties, late spring.

The furnishing, in the Art Deco style, is pale, simple and elegant

DARLING BOY, a good-looking young man, is stretched out on a chaise-longue, hidden behind a newspaper. He is in pyjamas bottoms, bare chested, his breakfast tray at his side. He wears a string of very large pearls.

CLÉA, at a desk, her head down, with her back to him, is doing the accounts.

> CLÉA
> *(Calls)* Anything in the papers?

> DARLING BOY
> Armandine is fancied for Longchamps. *(He turns a page.)* The Aga Khan has a new plaything.

A pause.

CLÉA turns, waving a bill at him. He looks at her in enquiry.

> CLÉA
> Twenty-four francs for an owl feather duster?

DARLING BOY
Hector says feathers are easier on the paintings. He's
worried about the impasto.

CLÉA bends over the bills.

DARLING BOY turns a page, reads, then sits up.

CLÉA
(Without turning) What?

DARLING BOY
Venezuelan Silver. Up 30 points!

CLÉA looks at him, crosses, and leans over his shoulder.

DARLING BOY
(Pointing) There! (They pore over the paper.) We'll
sell, now! No?

CLÉA
If they've struck a mother lode ...

DARLING BOY
The shares will go up and up!

CLÉA
It could be just a rumour.

DARLING BOY
Worth a punt though. Half?

CLÉA
A quarter. Give this to the chef. (Hands him an ornate
menu.) Tell him no crème surprise. Anyway, eggs give
you spots. They can have sorbets. And take off my
pearls.

He takes the pearls off from around his neck, and holds them in
his hand.

DARLING BOY

May I have them?

CLÉA

Why? What for?

DARLING BOY

Oh, no reason.

DARLING BOY throws down the pearls down, and exits with the menu.

CLÉA looks after him alertly, then crosses to the telephone.

CLÉA

Haussmann 425. M'sieu Perrault? It's Cléa. The Venezuelas. Sell a quarter ... Oui, bien sur. A bientôt. Merci.

DARLING BOY returns.

DARLING BOY

How much?

CLÉA

A quarter.

DARLING BOY

Good, we'll make ...

CLÉA

Two hundred and fifty thousand francs.

DARLING BOY

(Throws himself on the chaise-longue.) I'll buy the Bugatti.

CLÉA

No, you won't.

DARLING BOY

Why not?

CLÉA

You'll kill yourself.

DARLING BOY

A Suiza then. And Chanel for you.

CLÉA

Chanel? I'll look like a tennis player.

DARLING BOY

Good!

CLÉA

(*Head down at the accounts*) I must ring Nizza.

DARLING BOY

That old bag?

CLÉA

Nizza's not old! She was on every poster in Paris at one time! You should have seen her in the saddle. (*Sighs, reminiscent.*) Nizza, Queen of the Mustangs. And Blanche and her parakeets.

DARLING BOY

(*Laughs*) What happened to her?

CLÉA

Blanche? Ask your mother. She and Blanche were charioteers together.

DARLING BOY

You never told me that.

                    CLÉA

They drove four horses apiece! Well, till the collision.
She took to snake-charming after that.

CLÉA works.

DARLING BOY jumps up abruptly, crosses, and looks out of the window. She turns to observe him. He looks beautiful in the sunlight.

                    CLÉA

What's wrong?

                DARLING BOY

Nothing.

                    CLÉA

Good. I was right. The boxing's doing the trick.

He turns, biting his nails, and looks at her without smiling.

                    CLÉA

Stop biting your nails! When did you start that
again?

He crosses, stands over her, extending his hand.

                DARLING BOY

Do them for me?

She looks at him drily but fetches a little case. He sits on the chaise-longue, makes room for her at his side and she does his nails. He watches her.

                    CLÉA

How are things at Peloux's?

                DARLING BOY

Fine.

CLÉA

How's your mother?

DARLING BOY

Fine. She asked me to say she misses you. She says the poker sessions aren't the same.

CLÉA

She shouldn't be so quick with the accusations.

DARLING BOY

What do you expect? You keep taking her money.

CLÉA

And why would that be?

DARLING BOY

Because you're the better player.

CLÉA

Tell her to stick to bridge.

DARLING BOY

You'll be back. Miss all the charms of the banlieue? . . . the mayor, the undertaker, old Masseau poncing round with the coffee cups . . .

CLÉA

Leave Masseau alone. He's a dear friend. Divinely good-looking once. (*He glares at her.*) Not as beautiful as you, of course.

DARLING BOY

He's a shit. Last week Marie-Louise was his partner.

CLÉA

Marie-Louise? At your mother's? What was she doing there? You didn't tell me.

DARLING BOY

Forgot.

CLÉA

How is she, Madame Cobra? Still trying to pass for thirty? Another one ashamed of her own child. She's got a daughter, you know!

DARLING BOY

I heard.

He turns away, goes back to the window. He seems tense.

CLÉA

Why are you lunching with your mother? It can't be for the food.

DARLING BOY

That's my business. I don't ask about your private life.

CLÉA

Only because you're not interested.

DARLING BOY

I happen to have some discretion.

CLÉA

Rubbish. Your only interest is yourself.

DARLING BOY

Like everyone else!

CLÉA

There's no need to shout.

DARLING BOY

I'm sorry.

He comes and sits next to her, head down.

CLÉA

Darling Boy . . .

He does not respond.

CLÉA

What is it?

ROSE enters.

ROSE

Madame . . .

CLÉA

Thank you, Rose. (*To DARLING BOY*) He's here.

DARLING BOY

Who?

CLÉA

Monsieur Front. You haven't forgotten?

DARLING BOY

(*To ROSE*) Tell him to come back tomorrow.

CLÉA

Certainly not, that man has just crossed Paris for
you. Show him in, Rose.

ROSE goes.

CLÉA

What on earth is the matter with you? You adore
boxing.

DARLING BOY

Not today.

CLÉA

Why not?

DARLING BOY

I'm in a bad mood.

CLÉA

Good. You can take it out on Monsieur Front.

DARLING BOY

(*Gloomy*) Try hitting a brick wall, you mean?

He goes.

CLÉA laughs, crosses to her desk, and is about to sit down when MASSEAU enters, and looms up behind her.

CLÉA

Masseau! I wish you wouldn't creep in like that.

She lifts her arms, allowing him to kiss her briefly, and touch her face.

MASSEAU

I hope the time will never come when I have to knock, Cléa.

CLÉA

Sit down. You look dreadful. (*Crossing to the breakfast tray.*)

MASSEAU

That's because I haven't been to bed.

CLÉA

Well, don't boast about it.

MASSEAU

We went to the Turkish baths to recover.

CLÉA

(*Pouring him a large bowl of coffee.*) You look like wet blotting paper.

MASSEAU

Now, now. Too early for flattery. Thank you.

CLÉA

I remember when you'd drag a girl out of the Folies
Bergere, grab a horse and cart, and frighten the life
out of half of Paris.

MASSEAU

I was always a simple soul.

He blows on his coffee.

CLÉA

What do you want?

MASSEAU

It's about Friday. I've hired a barouche for drag night.
Are you coming? You missed the last one.

CLÉA

I had nothing to wear.

He looks at her, disbelieving.

CLÉA

Darling Boy fell asleep.

MASSEAU shrugs.

CLÉA

Was it fun?

MASSEAU

Outrageous. Old Lil danced on the table showing her
privates. And I won a hat.

CLÉA

Any good?

MASSEAU

No. I looked like an Englishman. Everyone was asking for you.

Laughter off.

DARLING BOY

(*Offstage*) Got you!

More laughter.

MASSEAU

What's going on?

CLÉA

It's Darling Boy's sparring lesson.

MASSEAU

Lesson?

CLÉA

With Monsieur Front. I'm paying for boxing lessons.

MASSEAU

Surely, he's ferocious enough already?

CLÉA

It uses up his energy. He's looking well.

MASSEAU

(*Massaging her neck*) Not as well as you, my dear.

CLÉA

You always did like the decrepit.

MASSEAU

(*Flash of jealousy*) What does Darling Boy like?

CLÉA

You'd better ask him, old thing.

MASSEAU

I hate it when you call me that.

CLÉA

Masseau!

MASSEAU

I'm still as jealous as a silly boy.

She lets him kiss her affectionately.

CLÉA

Not all boys are silly.

MASSEAU

Yes, they are. I was one myself.

CLÉA

Why so cruel about my changeling?

MASSEAU

You must allow me a little pique.

CLÉA

But you're a going concern, Masseau. Darling Boy
isn't.

MASSEAU

He's not?

CLÉA

He needs me.

MASSEAU

And he is, of course, delicious.

DARLING BOY enters in shirt and trousers, his hair wet.

DARLING BOY

Who's delicious?

CLÉA

What happened? Where's Monsieur Front?

DARLING BOY

I gave him a nosebleed.

MASSEAU

Congratulations.

CLÉA

You beat him? I told you if you kept up the training!
You look wonderful. He hasn't marked your face at all
this time. Let me look at you.

MASSEAU picks up his hat.

CLÉA

Masseau, are you going?

MASSEAU

Before I'm any more de trop. Shall we see you on
Friday?

CLÉA

Perhaps.

MASSEAU

Do try.

DARLING BOY

We'll let you know.

MASSEAU

Au 'voir, then.

MASSEAU goes. DARLING BOY grasps CLÉA.

DARLING BOY

Smell me.

CLÉA

(*Sniffs at his neck*) Guerlain?

DARLING BOY

If it's good enough for you . . .

CLÉA

But not by the bucketful. You'll bankrupt me. Stand still. (*She ties his tie.*) You'll be late for your lunch. (*Casually*) Who's going to be there?

DARLING BOY

Oh, the usual bores. Marie-Louise . . .

CLÉA

(*Puzzled*) Marie-Louise? Again?

The DOORBELL RINGS.

DARLING BOY flinches.

CLÉA

What's the matter?

He shakes his head.

ROSE enters, and whispers in CLÉA'S ear.

CLÉA looks surprised, and exits, followed by ROSE.

DARLING BOY looks after them warily.

CLÉA enters again.

CLÉA

Your mother's here!

DARLING BOY

(*Aghast*) My mother?

CLÉA

What can she want at this hour?

DARLING BOY

How the hell should I know? Where is she?

CLÉA

Down below. Rose is bringing her up. Is anything
wrong? Don't go!

But he goes.

ROSE enters.

ROSE

Madame Peloux, Madame.

CLÉA

And it is me she wants to see, not Darling Boy?

ROSE

She says you.

CLÉA

At eleven o'clock in the morning? (*She crosses to the
glass, renews her lipstick.*) It must be money. What
else could it be? She paid far too much for that place.
Do I need any powder?

ROSE

(*Inspects*) No, Madame. (*She straightens CLÉA'S
collar.*)

CLÉA

(*Sighs*) All right. Show her in.

ROSE goes.

CLÉA checks her hair in the mirror.

CHARLOTTE appears. She is Cléa's age, expensively dressed, but
without Cléa's style, and is overweight.

CHARLOTTE

Cléa!

CLÉA

Hullo, Charlotte.

CHARLOTTE

(*Stands back to inspect CLÉA*) Cléa! One look at you
and everything's forgotten.

CLÉA

Sit down.

CHARLOTTE

Oh, this outfit! (*Tugs at the hem of her skirt as she
sits.*) I don't think it suits me but others seem to like
it.

CLÉA

You look wonderful.

CHARLOTTE

Really? No, no, I don't count any more. I'm finished.
I'm no longer a woman, and d'you know? (*Lowers
her voice*) If you want the honest truth, I couldn't be
happier. (*Touches her crotch.*) All that fire in here?
Dead.

CLÉA

(*Cheerfully*) You won't be needing the hairbrush
then?

CHARLOTTE

There's no need to be vulgar, Cléa.

CLÉA

I'm only teasing.

CHARLOTTE

Cléa! You don't change. You're the same as twenty years ago. Same sense of fun.

CLÉA

What's the matter? Am I missed already?

CHARLOTTE

(*Awkwardly*) I haven't come about that.

Pause. She looks around.

CHARLOTTE

The boy not here?

CLÉA

In the cellar, counting the bottles.

CHARLOTTE

You see? I've given you a treasure! Well – loaned. What a beautiful room! Rose is a treasure. Who's the big oaf downstairs? The new manager? Any good?

CLÉA

Not good enough for you to pinch him off me. Cigarette?

CHARLOTTE demurs, then sighs and accepts.

CHARLOTTE

Bad for my poor heart, you know. I'm down to twenty a day. Brandy only on Saturday and Sunday. Well, at home. (*Sighs*) Our lovely Sundays, eh?

CLÉA

Let's just accept it, Charlotte.

CHARLOTTE

Oh, I don't give up so easily! We'll have our Peloux
Sundays again. Sooner than you think! Tennis,
picnics ...

CLÉA

Poker?

CHARLOTTE

(*Pause, stiff*) That's up to you, Cléa.

CLÉA

I really don't have the time these days.

CHARLOTTE

You will, before long. Are we alone?

CLÉA

Of course.

CHARLOTTE

Darling Boy's down below, you said?

CLÉA

Yes!

CHARLOTTE

Good. It's about him.

CLÉA

I had a feeling it might be.

CHARLOTTE

Yes. Well. (*Slight pause.*) As you know, Cléa, I've
always had my own style.

CLÉA

You have, Charlotte.

CHARLOTTE

My own – ambience . . .

CLÉA

I remember.

CHARLOTTE

(*Sighs*) Days of wine and roses, eh? Taking Darling
Boy to the park to sail his little boat and his choo-
choo train. Buying him picture books, tin soldiers . . .

CLÉA

Telling him Emil the abortionist was his uncle . . . the
girls his cousins from Cologne.

CHARLOTTE

I was trying to create a family atmosphere!

CLÉA

They gave him too many sweets.

CHARLOTTE

No, they didn't.

CLÉA

Yes, they did. They'd have ruined his teeth if I hadn't
stepped in.

CHARLOTTE

The girls adored him! I'm an en famille sort of person,
Cléa, and I make no apology for it. At heart, I'm just
an old-fashioned middle-class bourgeoise. There
were wild years, I admit, but they're all over now. A
respectable life has its advantages, you know.

CLÉA

Charlotte! You're not thinking of getting married?

CHARLOTTE

(*Trills with laughter*) Me? Me?! Well, one never knows! But not this time.

She leans forward, and puts a gloved hand on CLÉA's knee.

CHARLOTTE

Cléa my dearest, I am about to see all my dreams come true. Peace, prosperity – a family. Who knows? In time, some little angels?

CLÉA

Angels?

CHARLOTTE

(*Rises*) Come here! (*She embraces CLÉA, and sits down again.*) I have some news. Darling Boy . . .

CLÉA

Yes?

CHARLOTTE

I've arranged for Darling Boy to be married.

CLÉA sits very still.

CLÉA

Married? Congratulations. Does he know?

CHARLOTTE

He hasn't said anything to you?

CLÉA

No.

CHARLOTTE

Ah! The little beast. Keeping it to himself! He'll make me die laughing one of these days.

CLÉA

(*Impassive*) Yes, a comedian.

CHARLOTTE

Well, there was no hurry.

CLÉA

Really?

CHARLOTTE

Good heavens, we don't plan to get these children wed
before – well, not for six weeks at least.

CLÉA

Who is 'we'?

CHARLOTTE

Marie-Louise and me, of course.

CLÉA

Marie-Louise? The everlastingly lovely
Marie-Louise?

CHARLOTTE

Yes! It's her daughter – Edmée!

CLÉA

Edmée? That little thing? What are you talking
about? She's fourteen years old.

CHARLOTTE

Was, my sweet. Not anymore. Edmée is eighteen
years of age. She doesn't have my looks, but she's a
charming little thing ... a princess. You can see that.

CLÉA

I wouldn't know. (*Lies back, smoking*)

CHARLOTTE

To see life opening up for a sweet young girl as she's
entrusted to the arms of my own Darling Boy ... What
are you laughing at?

CLÉA

Life opening up for a girl handed over to him? You
might as well throw a rabbit to a stoat.

CHARLOTTE

How can you say such things? He is kind, gentle

CLÉA

You'd know that, would you?

CHARLOTTE

I am his mother.

CLÉA

Since when?

CHARLOTTE, offended, doesn't answer.

CLÉA

Come on, Charlotte. There's nobody here. Since when
have you been his mother?

CHARLOTTE

My dear, you're upset. I've upset you. I'm sorry, Cléa.
Oh, I'm so cross with myself! How could I have been
so clumsy? I should have taken it gently, not come
crashing in. I do understand. A shock like that ...

CLÉA

Shock? I'm not shocked, Charlotte. I've been
expecting this. Since I first started taking him about
so that he wasn't left to the servants for months on
end.

CHARLOTTE

(*Soppy*) You bought him his first velvet suit,
remember? He looked so beautiful, like something out
of a picture book. Remember when I put him in the
Flower Festival? All naked among the roses?

CLÉA

His feet were dirty. You knew I could never pass a
stray dog. You saw me coming. Every time I took him
from you, he was thin and miserable. And every time
you got him back, he was glowing.

CHARLOTTE

That's not fair.

CLÉA

It's the truth. You can have him back, Charlotte. Debt,
drugs and alcohol free. I would even say he does me
proud – well – except . . .

CHARLOTTE

Except what?

CLÉA

You never know with him, do you? Which way he's
going to jump. (*Laughs*) At least he's not predictable.
She'll have her work cut out.

CHARLOTTE

Edmée? Yes, obviously. But there are ways . . .

CLÉA

How do you mean?

CHARLOTTE

If you're a young woman.

CLÉA

I daresay.

CHARLOTTE

Poor boy.

CLÉA

Why?

CHARLOTTE

I'm not reproaching you, Cléa dear, I wouldn't dream of it. But, well, he's never had time to lead the life of a bachelor has he, poor boy? And now we're both losing him. Of course, she is enchanting.

CLÉA

Good. I hope he's awash with love. So, is that all, Charlotte dear? I do have a hotel to run.

CHARLOTTE

I thought, under the circumstances ...

CLÉA

You didn't honestly think I'd be upset? Charlotte! I've been waiting for you to find a good match for him. Take him off my hands.

CHARLOTTE

Oh, what a relief! Naturally, I mean, you've been à deux for five years. It's bound to be a blow. We've dreaded telling you.

CLÉA

"We?"

CHARLOTTE

Tho darling boy and me. He cares for you, Cléa. A
great deal. Naturally, he's worried that his leaving
will be – well – an upset.

CLÉA

(*Laughs*) My dear, that is <u>so</u> sentimental. You talk as
if we were in love!

CHARLOTTE

(*Draws in breath*) Oh! Oh, what a relief. I'm nothing
but a romantic fool – but there you are. I am his
mother and he <u>is</u> irresistible. We've always agreed on
that. Come here, give me a hug! Let me look at you.
Ah, soignée as ever! We must go shopping. There's
nothing like spending money to lift the spirits. As
soon as the lovebirds are cooing away in Italy, we'll
get back to our Sundays. (*She bangs CLÉA on the
shoulder.*) Our mad Sundays, eh? We've missed you . . .

Despite herself CLÉA groans. CHARLOTTE embraces CLÉA again.

CHARLOTTE

Ooh, you smell good. Jicky?

CLÉA

As ever.

CHARLOTTE

Lovely. Perfume sinks in better when the skin starts
to go. Have you noticed?

She picks up her bag and gloves.

CHARLOTTE

I'll send round the wedding invite as soon as it's
printed.

She goes.

CLÉA

(*Calls after her*) I look forward to it!

Alone, she seems on the point of collapse.

DARLING BOY enters upstage and watches her.

She turns, and they look at each other.

DARLING BOY

Has she gone?

CLÉA turns away.

CLÉA

Why didn't you tell me?

DARLING BOY

She thought it should come from her.

CLÉA

You were afraid. You got her to do it for you.

Silence.

DARLING BOY

I didn't want to hurt you.

CLÉA

Why have I never been able to stop you from lying? Perhaps you _were_ worried? With you it's impossible to tell. Surely, you've known me long enough to trust me?

DARLING BOY

I do trust you.

CLÉA

Not onough, it seems. I deserved better. That you should want to leave me – find someone younger. That's inevitable. I've even been looking around for some nice rich girl.

DARLING BOY

Are you joking?

CLÉA

Between Charlotte and me you haven't exactly been exposed to steady domestic bliss. Perhaps that's what you need.

DARLING BOY

So why are you looking like that?

CLÉA

Because you disappoint. Are you going to tell me about her? Is she rich? A good dowry?

He writes down a sum. She puts on her glasses, reads it.

CLÉA

I've known better.

DARLING BOY

There may be more from her father.

CLÉA

Which one?

He shrugs.

CLÉA

So. You'll be all right for money. Plus, what you've salted away here for the past five years.

He slides to the floor, and rests his head on her knees.

                    DARLING BOY
    I've been worth it, haven't I?

She bends tenderly behind him, then checks herself.

                    CLÉA
    Tell me about Edmée. Is she nice looking?

DARLING BOY shrugs.

                    CLÉA
    Intelligent?

                    DARLING BOY
    We'll see.

                    CLÉA
    Don't you know?

                    DARLING BOY
    I'll find out. I'm marrying her, aren't I?

Behind him, CLÉA'S head goes down in pain.

She pulls herself together.

                    CLÉA
    And she loves you?

                    DARLING BOY
    She says so.

                    CLÉA
    What about you?

                    DARLING BOY
    Never mind about me. What about you?

                    CLÉA
    Me?

DARLING BOY

What are you going to do?

CLÉA

What do you want me to do? Become a nun? Get fat
because you're leaving me? Is that what you want?

DARLING BOY

Yes.

Silence.

CLÉA

Poor baby. So, I lose a young lover – change one
wicked boy for another. It won't be the first time.

DARLING BOY

I know that, and I don't care. I don't care that I wasn't
the first. What I want is to be the last.

CLÉA

You want your leaving to finish me off? Sorry, my
dear. Admittedly you're not a passing fancy like the
others. You're my project. The stray that I rescued
and fed and ... (*But she cannot go on.*) Ring for Rose,
would you?

DARLING BOY

(*Alarmed*) What for?

CLÉA

(*Smiles brightly*) She can put your things together,
have them sent over to L'Hotel Peloux.

DARLING BOY

Why?

CLÉA

You can't expect to do your courting from this house.

DARLING BOY

Why not?

CLÉA

Sending flowers from my telephone? Put your jacket
on. We're going out.

DARLING BOY

Where?

CLÉA

To buy you a wedding present! What would you like?

DARLING BOY

(*Playing her at her own game, thinks*) A pearl tie-
pin. A really big one. No, wait. I've seen a cigarette
case in white jade, with the edge set in diamonds.

CLÉA

I see, something really discreet and enough to
bankrupt me. Come on.

She helps him on with his jacket,

CLÉA

I'm going to be <u>so</u> well off when you're gone. I'll be able
to afford dowries for all your children.

DARLING BOY

(*Laughs*) Great. You can be godmother to the first
boy.

He follows her out. We hear them laugh, off. A door closes.

Fade to black.

ACT ONE – SCENE TWO

The garden of L'Hotel Peloux, a few weeks later.

A large parasol is open on the grass over an ornate garden seat.

The sounds of a tennis game, off.

EDMÉE, in tennis clothes, enters. She wanders about, and gazes this way and that, looking for someone. She turns her head, seeing someone coming, sits under the parasol, stretching out, as if at ease.

MASSEAU enters. He bears a tray with a jug of lemon squash and a glass.

MASSEAU

I thought you might be thirsty.

EDMÉE

Thank you – I am!

He pours a drink for her.

EDMÉE

Thank you.

MASSEAU

Not at all. Sweets to the sweet.

EDMÉE sits up and drinks. Sounds of the tennis game. They gaze offstage.

EDMÉE'S gaze wanders.

MASSEAU

He went over to the lake.

EDMÉE

Ah.

MASSEAU

You mustn't think anything of it. He's like that.

EDMÉE

I know.

Enter DARLING BOY.

They both look up. DARLING BOY looms over them. MASSEAU gets the message.

MASSEAU

Au 'voir. I must attend to my duties as sommelier.

He goes.

EDMÉE

What's the matter?

DARLING BOY shrugs and moves away.

EDMÉE

Why? What have I said?

DARLING BOY

(*Shrugs*) If you need to ask.

EDMÉE

Fred, I'm not a mind reader.

Silence.

DARLING BOY

If you must know, I'm avoiding our hostess, Madame Peloux.

EDMÉE

Why do you call her that?

DARLING BOY

It's her name.

EDMÉE

She's your mother! *(Slight pause.)* You were very rude to her.

DARLING BOY

Almost as bad as you with Marie-Louise.

EDMÉE

I'm always very polite with Maman.

DARLING BOY

Exactly.

EDMÉE

We hardly ever meet, Fred. When she does call, it's usually to introduce a new father.

DARLING BOY

Mine were always Uncles.

They laugh.

He throws himself down, and puts his hands behind his head.

EDMÉE

You get used to being on your own.

DARLING BOY

I never did.

EDMÉE

How did you manage?

DARLING BOY

By making myself extremely attractive.

EDMÉE

. . . and lovable . . .

DARLING BOY

Not lovable. Attractive. It's not the same thing.

EDMÉE

(*Slight pause.*) Were you moved round a lot?

DARLING BOY

Yes.

EDMÉE

There are advantages to that.

DARLING BOY

Such as?

EDMÉE

It's very educational. You pick things up.

DARLING BOY

You mean, like how to mix drinks . . .

EDMÉE

Make pasta, darn ballet shoes . . .

DARLING BOY

Shoe horses.

EDMÉE

(*Laughs*) Shoe horses?

DARLING BOY

A friend used to take me to the country.

Slight pause. She sits, her arms round her knees.

EDMÉE

I used to keep snails.

DARLING BOY

(*Astonished*) So did I!

EDMÉE

In a shoe box. I painted their shells. Did you?

> DARLING BOY

No. I trod on them.

She swipes at him.

> DARLING BOY

I put one in the pot au feu once – in a hotel restaurant.

> EDMÉE

What happened?

> DARLING BOY

I was asked to apologise.

> EDMÉE

Did you?

> DARLING BOY

No.

Silence.

> EDMÉE

Funny we both kept snails.

> DARLING BOY

Yes.

> EDMÉE

They're so dignified.

He laughs, making her lose face.

> EDMÉE

What?

> DARLING BOY

You're funny.

He jumps up, gives her his hand. She looks up at him. He regards her, and decides he wants to kiss her.

They embrace. Then she throws her arms around him joyously. He is surprised and laughs. She smiles at him and goes.

He follows her off, thoughtful.

Fade to black.

ACT ONE – SCENE THREE

Cléa's salon. Late morning.

CHARLOTTE enters, weighed down with expensive shopping bags. She is followed by MASSEAU, laden, who shrugs in apology to ROSE.

>   ROSE
> Desolée, Madame Peloux, but Madame is not at home.

>   CHARLOTTE
> Ouf, I'm exhausted! How long will she be?

>   ROSE
> I couldn't say, Madame.

CHARLOTTE waves ROSE away dismissively.

>   CHARLOTTE
> (*To MASSEAU*) I need to know if she'll lend me Hector
> and two of the maids. I can never keep mine. Well,
> not being behind the Rue St Honoré. But I prefer the
> Faubourg. The fresh air. (*She calls*) Rose!

ROSE appears.

>   CHARLOTTE
> Put these in water for Cléa, I saw them in the market.

ROSE takes the droopy bunch, looks at it, and puts it to one side.

CHARLOTTE

Brandy, Masseau?

MASSEAU

(*Looks at his watch*) Thank you no, I have a luncheon
engagement.

CHARLOTTE

Did you speak to your tailor?

MASSEAU

My tailor?

CHARLOTTE

About the weskits for the ushers. Tell him to give me
a price today. Oh, I must sit down, walking is so bad
for the legs.

ROSE brings her a drink. She drinks.

CHARLOTTE

That's better. (*Indicates for ROSE to top up her glass,
then waves her away.*)

ROSE goes.

CHARLOTTE

I'm full of fizz! I can hardly keep still I'm so excited!
The marriage of my only child, Masseau. My son!

MASSEAU

A milestone. A happy milestone.

CHARLOTTE

And this lovely weather! Do you find it sets you up?

MASSEAU

In what way, Charlotte?

CHARLOTTE

You know, as I came out of Patou's, a man crossed the
street and started to follow me. I was even tempted
for a moment. Was that dreadful of me?

MASSEAU

Not at all. *(Calls)* Rose!

ROSE enters.

MASSEAU

When are you expecting Madame?

ROSE

Not until after lunch, Monsieur.

CHARLOTTE

I can't wait that long. I have caterers and
dressmakers to see. I hope Cléa can spare <u>you</u>,
Masseau. It's a waste of time talking to Fred.

CLÉA appears in a kimono.

CHARLOTTE

I was saying, Cléa, it's useless trying to talk to Fred.
He's in another world.

CLÉA

(Lighting a cigarette.) What do you want?

CHARLOTTE

I need you to do the menus for the wedding breakfast,
and put up some of the guests. Fred's school friends,
I don't want them underfoot, eating me out of house
and home. Oh, and I'll need Hector and a couple of the
maids, and what are you going to wear? Goodness, my
hands, I must have an oil treatment before the day.
Would you believe, Masseau, that these were once

called the loveliest hands in Europe? Alphonse the
Twolfth drank champagne from these very palms. He
called them his little pearl shells.

CLÉA

(*Laughs*) Yes, well, being a King is no guarantee of
wit.

CHARLOTTE

Now. What about it?

CLÉA

About what?

CHARLOTTE

I'm thinking cerise. My dressmaker is going mad
with suspense. I keep changing my mind.

CLÉA

What about the little one?

CHARLOTTE

The little one?

CLÉA

The bride. What will she be wearing?

CHARLOTTE

White of course. They'll see to all that. I thought
perhaps a soft salmon – with a bolero.

MASSEAU

No. No bolero.

CHARLOTTE

Why not? Oh well, first I need to know what Cléa's
coming in so's we don't clash. By the way, Fred would
like a nice little cabin cruiser as a wedding present.
He said not to say anything but, well . . .

CLÉA

He shall have it.

CHARLOTTE

And you'll be wearing?

CLÉA

Charlotte, you can't really expect me to be present at
Darling Boy's wedding.

CHARLOTTE

Why ever not?

CLÉA

It won't do.

CHARLOTTE

But you must!

MASSEAU

Surely it will be more comme il faut for Cléa not to
appear ...

CHARLOTTE

Of course, you must come. You're my closest friend.
Everybody knows we've always shared him. Now.
What about the hat? It's not that I want mine bigger
but, after all, I am the mother of the groom. Anyway,
Marie-Louise will probably put both our noses out of
joint parading her bosoms.

MASSEAU

They are magnificent.

CHARLOTTE

So, have you decided on your ensemble?

CLÉA

Charlotte. Settle for the cabin cruiser. You must do
without me.

CHARLOTTE

But that'll spoil everything! People need to see you
there!

CLÉA

No. This wedding is your affair. Marriages have
nothing to do with me, nor I with them.

CHARLOTTE

You're doing it on purpose! You're trying to spoil …

CLÉA

No, I'm not.

CHARLOTTE

Anyway, how am I to see to it all on my own? I can't
see to everything!

CLÉA

What about Marie-Louise?

CHARLOTTE

We're not speaking. That bitch is too mean to pay for
even one bridesmaid. She's spending all the money
on herself. (*To MASSEAU*) Do something! Talk her
round. Make her change her mind.

MASSEAU shrugs and turns away. She turns to CLÉA.

CHARLOTTE

Are you coming or not? (*Silence.*) It's Darling Boy's
wedding!

Silence. CHARLOTTE looks from one to the other, then grabs her
bags and the flowers.

MASSEAU ushers her out.

CHARLOTTE

(*Going*) Poodle!

Silence.

CLÉA

Masseau, will you do something for me?

MASSEAU

Anything.

CLÉA

Put me on a train to somewhere.

MASSEAU

As you wish.

CLÉA

Today.

He nods. She approaches, takes his hands.

CLÉA

Look after him for me.

MASSEAU

I'll do my best.

CLÉA

He'll need someone.

They look at each other. She turns to go.

CLÉA

Tell her she can have Hector.

She exits.

MASSEAU

You will write?

ROSE is at the door.

MASSEAU

You heard?

ROSE

Oui, Monsieur.

MASSEAU

You will go with her?

ROSE

(*Shakes her head*) She says not.

MASSEAU

She shouldn't be alone. If anything happened to
her ...

ROSE

(*Low*) If anything happened to her, I'd kill myself.

MASSEAU

Then we must be sure that it doesn't – for both our
sakes.

Fade to black.

ACT ONE – SCENE FOUR

The foyer of a spa, with elegant furniture and Kentia palms. The
sound of a trio.

CLÉA is sitting alone, a tray of tea before her.

MASSEAU appears.

CLÉA

Masseau!

MASSEAU

May I? (*He sits across from her.*)

CLÉA

What are you doing here?

MASSEAU

Don't worry, all is well.

CLÉA

Tea?

MASSEAU

Thank you.

CLÉA

(*Pouring*) When did you arrive?

MASSEAU

This morning.

CLÉA

You must try the mud baths.

MASSEAU

Anything to oblige.

CLÉA

You can oblige me by taking the next train back to
Paris.

MASSEAU

I thought you might need me.

CLÉA

For what? Why should I want to see you?

MASSEAU rises.

MASSEAU

I'm sorry. I'll go.

CLÉA

(*Snarls*) Oh sit down. Now you're here you may as well
spill the beans. It's what you came for, isn't it? What
did she wear in the end?

He sits again, and drinks tea.

MASSEAU

Cream and tobacco satin, striped and pleated from
the hip.

CLÉA

(*Winces*) And the bad diamonds, I suppose.

MASSEAU

No. The jet parure.

CLÉA

Really? Was that you?

MASSEAU

(*Shakes his head*) Fred. He refused to leave the house
until she toned it down.

Despite herself, CLÉA laughs.

CLÉA

Wicked boy. What about the hat?

He shakes his head.

MASSEAU

Pink roses. And birds.

CLÉA

Birds?

MASSEAU

With beaks. Her milliner's geste de saison.

CLÉA

Open or closed?

MASSEAU

Gaping. To celebrate fertility.

Silence as they savour this. The silence deepens.

CLÉA

And the little one?

MASSEAU

Like a sacrificial offering. No jewels or train, just a
chaplet of flowers.

CLÉA

Was there a choir? Darling Boy likes church music.

MASSEAU

No. The ceremony was very short. It was as if they
wanted to seal the bargain before . . .

CLÉA

. . . before he changed his mind.

Silence.

MASSEAU

The ring was on her finger without a glance.

Silence.

CLÉA

(*Quietly*) Masseau, do me the favour of leaving before
I push this fork in your face.

He rises.

At the exit he stands, watching her. And leaves.

Light change to night.

CLÉA sits, immobile.

On the other side of the stage, EDMÉE and DARLING BOY, on honeymoon, are on a balcony overlooking a moonlit sea. He stands by the balcony, gazing out to sea.

EDMÉE, immobile, watches his back.

Fade to black.

ACT TWO

ACT TWO – SCENE ONE

At Charlotte's.

The decor is dreadful. The sound of VOICES.

CHARLOTTE enters, and crosses quickly with a large vase of flowers. She returns and exits, trilling a song. Then she enters, consulting her notebook.

> CHARLOTTE
>
> (*Calls to staff offstage*) Hortense! Hortense! Has Francoise made the bed?

> VOICE
>
> (*Off*) Oui Madame Peloux.

> CHARLOTTE
>
> With the Duke of Siena's sheets?

> VOICE
>
> Oui, Madame.

> CHARLOTTE
>
> And the flowers?

> VOICE
>
> Oui, Madame.

> CHARLOTTE
>
> Well, send Emil out to open the gates. What's the time? (*She looks at her watch-necklace.*) Heavens! They'll be here if the train is on time. (*Calls*) Hortense! Did you speak to the chef?

268

VOICE

Oui, Madame.

CHARLOTTE

And he knows about the riz a l'Italienne?

VOICE

Oui, Madame.

CHARLOTTE, placated, straightens her frilled jacket.

She puts a large silk flower in her button-hole, crosses to her handbag, takes out scent and sprays herself. She spits on her finger and smoothes her eyelashes, pulls down her corset, then flops into a chair, and throws off her uncomfortable high-heeled shoes. She heaves a sigh and rests her head against the back of the chair, humming. The humming stops as she dozes off. She jerks awake at the triple hoot of a CAR HORN.

It is repeated as she hops about, putting on her shoes.

CHARLOTTE

(*Calls*) They're here! Hortense! Francoise! Antoine! They're here!

She dashes off. The sound of VOICES.

DARLING BOY enters, pale and unsmiling.

Enter CHARLOTTE, taking his coat, followed by EDMÉE.

CHARLOTTE

Darling boy! Welcome home! Give your Mama a big kiss! (*She tries to embrace him.*)

DARLING BOY

Where is Antoine?

CHARLOTTE

Bringing in the luggage. Let me look at you. The lovebirds! *(She hugs EDMÉE.)* Ooh! filling out already! And so fresh after all that travelling!

EDMÉE

We stopped overnight in Lyon. Fred was tired.

Sounds of luggage being brought in, offstage.

CHARLOTTE goes to the door and calls.

CHARLOTTE

Up the stairs to the Empress suite!

DARLING BOY

Don't let them open the trunks.

CHARLOTTE

Why not?

EDMÉE

Why, Fred?

DARLING BOY

I'm only staying overnight.

CHARLOTTE

But I've changed everything round for you.

More noises, off. DARLING BOY exits swiftly.

EDMÉE

Fred!

CHARLOTTE

Take no notice, dear. He just likes to grumble. He's keeping his smiles for you.

EDMÉE

(Doubtfully) Yes.

CHARLOTTE

Be patient. It's early days. Does he bother you much
at night? Don't worry, it'll wear off. As I always tell
virgins – just let the man take the lead. And laugh at
his jokes, of course.

EDMÉE

Jokes?

CHARLOTTE

Always be a good listener. Men do like to be admired.

EDMÉE

Thank you. May I ring Maman?

CHARLOTTE

You can, but you won't get her. She's in Cairo. No
bridesmaids! If there's one thing I can't stand it's
meanness. Never mind, you were better on your own.
There's always one bridesmaid who looks prettier
than the bride. Are you feeling all right?

EDMÉE

If I could just . . .

CHARLOTTE

Of course. Everything's ready for you, including silk
sheets. Dinner at eight.

EDMÉE goes. CHARLOTTE trills.

DARLING BOY enters.

CHARLOTTE

She's looking a little washed out.

DARLING BOY

Who?

CHARLOTTE

Who?! Your bride! Who did you think I meant?

DARLING BOY

Has anyone asked for me?

CHARLOTTE

No, we didn't expect you back so soon.

DARLING BOY

No messages?

CHARLOTTE

From Cléa you mean? Heavens no. She's been
cavorting on the Riviera. It's in all the columns.
There's a new man. Well, she needs consolation. She'll
have put her hand in her pocket, I daresay.

DARLING BOY

She's not in Paris?

CHARLOTTE

Came back yesterday. I meant to ring. Ask her over.
But I thought no. After all, she's not family. I must see
to the duck. I'm using Cléa's recipe. I know you like it.

DARLING BOY

(*Warningly*) Now, now, Madame Peloux . . .

CHARLOTTE

What? What did I say?

DARLING BOY

Nothing. Go and stir something.

She goes.

He stands, motionless. EDMÉE comes in.

EDMÉE

Come and see upstairs. It's amazing.

DARLING BOY

Madame Peloux been putting bells on the bedclothes?
(*He looks round*) God, this house is ugly.

EDMÉE

You wanted to be here. As soon as we got to Florence
you said we had to come home.

DARLING BOY

Home yes. This isn't home.

EDMÉE

That's because we're early. The builders haven't
finished. By next week we'll be under our own roof.

He moves away abruptly.

EDMÉE

What's the matter?

He stands, his back to her.

EDMÉE

Darling Boy?

DARLING BOY

(*He turns, savage.*) Don't call me that!

He exits.

EDMÉE wanders over to Darling Boy's briefcase. Despite herself,
she is curious. She begins to browse, going through his papers.

DARLING BOY enters behind her.

DARLING BOY

What are you doing?

EDMÉE

(Jumps) Nothing. I was waiting for you.

DARLING BOY

Do you want to see them? *(He nods at the papers in her hand.)*

EDMÉE

Of course not.

DARLING BOY

Go ahead.

EDMÉE

I'm not interested in your old love letters.

DARLING BOY

I don't have any old love letters. Take a look! *(He grabs some papers, and offers them.)* Receipts. Bills. More bills. Listen to this: "My dearest ... " Oh, it's from Madame Peloux.

Laughing, he throws the papers at her, and sits. EDMÉE picks up one of the papers.

DARLING BOY

What's that?

EDMÉE

Nothing. It's just ... *(But her voice falters. She reads)* "I'm not bored, I'm being good and taking my treatments till you arrive ... "

He jumps up.

EDMÉE

"... maybe through the window, throwing off your clothes, my darling savage."

DARLING BOY

Give me that! (*He grabs the letter.*)

EDMÉE

I don't need to read the signature. I know who it is.
(*She sits and weeps.*)

DARLING BOY

Come on … don't cry. What's all the fuss about?

EDMÉE

Go away, I hate the sight of you!

DARLING BOY

What's the matter? What have I done?

EDMÉE

You don't love me. You've never loved me! You think I
don't see things? I've had enough! (*She sits weeping
and mopping her eyes.*)

DARLING BOY

You're mad.

EDMÉE

I wish I were. Mad people live in another world.
It can't be worse than this one. Oh, this room, it's
horrible.

DARLING BOY

You don't have to stay here.

EDMÉE

No. It wouldn't trouble you if I walked out of that door
this minute! If you're not being rude, you're ignoring
me. Do you think I don't know who you're thinking of
all the time?

DARLING BOY steps back as if slapped.

DARLING BOY

(*After a pause*) You've been keeping that to yourself.
(*He walks about.*)

EDMÉE

Fred, I'm sorry.

DARLING BOY

Don't be. You haven't upset me. It's better like this.

EDMÉE

You see, you admit it!

DARLING BOY

(*With a kind of innocence*) But of course.

EDMÉE

(*Beginning to cry again*) Then why did you marry
me?

DARLING BOY

(*Thinks*) How should I know?

DARLING BOY

Now don't spoil it.

EDMÉE

I want you to love me and you love that old woman!

DARLING BOY

Yes, she's old! Older than you. Old enough to be my
mother – take care of me. The best thing I've ever had
in my life. Till now.

She glares at him.

EDMÉE

Go back to her then!

DARLING BOY

It's all very well to say that.

EDMÉE

If you miss her so much ...

DARLING BOY

I'm not used to being without her! It hurts.

EDMÉE

You can say this? To me?

DARLING BOY

Who else should I say it to?

EDMÉE

Ohh!

DARLING BOY

If I can't tell you ... You're always talking about trust.
About being open. Now that I ...

EDMÉE

You're monstrous. A monster!

DARLING BOY

Because I'm telling the truth? What do you want from
me? Have I been out of your sight for the last five
weeks? Have I slept in a separate room – in a separate
bed?

EDMÉE

And that's a proof of love?

DARLING BOY

Better than calling me a liar and dishonest, and
everything else you're throwing at me. Is that love?

EDMÉE

(*Humbly*) No. It's jealousy.

DARLING BOY

And that's supposed to excuse everything? You don't
want me to lie, but you don't want the truth. You want
me to forget everything and everybody I knew before
you . . .

EDMÉE

Yes!

DARLING BOY

. . . whether or not they've been good to me, looked
after me . . .

EDMÉE

Oh, say her name! What can it do to me now?

DARLING BOY

There's no need for you to . . . it's the way you . . .
There's no respect for her.

EDMÉE

Then go back there, while she's still got a few years
left!

DARLING BOY

And you're eighteen, with white skin and hair all
over the pillow. I suppose you think that's unique?

EDMÉE

Oh, Fred. That's the last thing you'll ever say to me. I
want a separation. A divorce.

DARLING BOY

Come on . . .

ACT TWO

EDMÉE

I mean it.

DARLING BOY

And what would that solve?

EDMÉE

Everything. I don't care. Just let me go.

DARLING BOY

It won't solve anything.

EDMÉE

Why not?

DARLING BOY

Because you love me. It's not your fault.

EDMÉE

Oh Fred! I don't want to leave you ...

DARLING BOY

Of course you don't.

The sound of a BELL.

EDMÉE

What's that?

DARLING BOY

Madame Peloux, ringing the dinner bell.

EDMÉE

Already? Oh, I look awful! Don't go in without me.
Promise? Wait for me. I'll only be a minute. (*At the
door*) You'll be here?

She kisses him on the cheek, and goes quickly.

Alone, DARLING BOY stands, abstracted for a long moment. He
walks up and down, then suddenly grabs his coat and goes.

A pause.

EDMÉE enters. She looks around.

> EDMÉE

Fred?

> Light change.

ACT TWO – SCENE TWO

Cléa's salon, later the same evening.

CLÉA and MASSEAU are sitting – a pedestal table between them – with coffee and liqueurs. CLÉA is smoking with a cigarette holder, her elbow on the arm of the chair.

MASSEAU is doing his embroidery.

> MASSEAU

(Undertone, counting stitches) One, two, three, four, five ...

> CLÉA

Masseau! I forgot to give you a drink! Would you like one?

> MASSEAU

(Nods) ... nine ... (mutters, then) I'm sorry, my dear, there's a little blue reindeer demanding my attention. The detail in this tapestry is maddening. (Takes off his glasses.) I'd love an armagnac.

CLÉA leans over, and looks at his embroidery.

> CLÉA

Mmm. You're so clever.

He smiles up at her.

MASSEAU

A cushion for Charlotte. She needs four.

CLÉA

(*Looks at the cushion*) Four?

MASSEAU

A commission. (*Glum*) Her design.

CLÉA

(*Neutral*) Yes.

MASSEAU

I'll do just the one.

He bends to his sewing, and watches her as she moves about restlessly.

CLÉA

I should pack.

MASSEAU

Must you go?

CLÉA

Oh, I think so. Not that there isn't plenty to do here.
Did I tell you, I've been offered a share in a racehorse!

She moves about restlessly, then stops.

CLÉA

I can't breathe the same air.

MASSEAU

In the end one has to ...

CLÉA

Bite the bullet? Yes, of course. But not yet. I thought
Sicily.

MASSEAU

(*Pricks his finger.*) Ow! Sorry. (*He sucks his finger.*)
We went to Sicily – remember?

CLÉA

Of course I remember.

MASSEAU

You were bored.

CLÉA

What a memory! Perhaps Spain.

MASSEAU

The last time you came back from Spain you could
hardly walk.

CLÉA

Liar. When I behave badly, it's at home in a decent
bed, and all the comforts. I'll probably settle for
Antibes.

MASSEAU

Antibes?

CLÉA

Why not? I can talk to the old women in the lobbies.
And the old men will tell me stories, and carry my
things, and we'll both know it's a waste of time.

MASSEAU

Thank you.

CLÉA

I didn't mean you! I met a retired Colonel in St Jean
de Luz. Impressive, like a decorated cliff face.

MASSEAU

But past it?

CLÉA

I never found out. He was wearing a corset.

MASSEAU

Sounds delightful.

CLÉA laughs. Pause.

CLÉA

I've been a fool, keeping a lover for five years. I should have gone in for passades – litte adventures.

MASSEAU

These things don't always arrange themselves.

CLÉA

Five years with the same man? It's like being marooned in the colonies, and coming back and no-one knows you anymore, and you've forgotten how to dress.

MASSEAU

Oh, you mustn't do that – forget how to dress.

CLÉA

You mean <u>you'd</u> abandon me?

MASSEAU

Because you wouldn't be Cléa.

CLÉA

I'll make sure my seams are straight.

MASSEAU

(*Slight pause*) It's going to take time.

CLÉA

I know. What I feel for that boy – why should it be any less because he's young enough to be my son? It's

probably the reason for it. That's something you'll
never know. The pain of not having a child when it's
too late. You think – oh, perhaps next year, or I'll keep
the next one. Then it's too late. What, for so long, you
didn't want, you now can't have. Ever.

She sits. MASSEAU looks across at her bent head.

> CLÉA

I sent him a note.

> MASSEAU

A note?

> CLÉA

I said goodbye. Farewell from a tired old mistress to a
vicious young lover.

> MASSEAU

It was his choice.

> CLÉA

Was it? (*Rises*) I shouldn't have cut him off.

> MASSEAU

Why not?

> CLÉA

Because he's not ready for it. I took away his
protection. If I'd been really chic, I'd have made a man
of him instead of thinking only of myself.

> MASSEAU

You've given that boy everything. You've cared for
him as he will care for his children. It's a one- way
path, not a game of tennis. Your job's been to throw
love at him. You've done that.

CLÉA

I'm not his mother.

MASSEAU

Aren't you? Cléa, the important thing is not to be
loved, but to be allowed to love.

CLÉA suddenly leaps to her feet.

CLÉA

What I cannot stand is this empty house!

MASSEAU

Empty? The guests are here, the staff is here … I'm
here.

CLÉA

I'll go away for a while. Who knows? New horizons,
new wardrobe, new diet. I don't think I can come back
here. Live here. Not anymore.

She crosses, and gazes at herself in the glass for a long moment.

MASSEAU

Then sell. Sell the hotel.

CLÉA

But what would I do? Where would I go? What for?
What does it matter? (*Silence.*) I miss him. I miss him
in my bed.

MASSEAU moves, scraping his chair. He tries to put his sewing
into his embroidery bag without success, irritating CLÉA.

CLÉA

What's the matter? Masseau?

He does not reply but sits with his head bent. She crosses and
stands over him.

CLÉA

Are you crying?

MASSEAU

No.

CLÉA

Why are you crying? Oh, for heaven's sake, I shan't be
away forever.

MASSEAU rises, hugs her fervently and stumbles off.

She lifts his embroidery bag, but he has gone.

ROSE enters with a valise.

CLÉA

Poor Masseau. Why do I treat him so badly?

ROSE

Because he wishes it, Madam.

CLÉA

Oh Rose! Did you find my new ring?

ROSE

It was in the crocodile box.

She hands the ring box to CLÉA, who takes out the ring and puts it
on. They both murmur approval.

CLÉA

What do you think?

ROSE

Oh Madame – now that is an emerald!

CLÉA

Good colour eh? (*They pore over the ring.*) You'd
better put it in the safe. No, I'll keep it on for now.

ROSE puts the ring box in her pocket, begins to pack the valise with books and the diary from Cléa's table. CLÉA watches.

CLÉA

Rose . . .

ROSE

Madame?

CLÉA

Things aren't going to be the same from now on. If you feel like making a change, I'd understand.

ROSE

(On her knees, looks up, stricken) You mean, leave you, Madame?

CLÉA

I'm not thinking of myself. But if life becomes quieter . . .

ROSE

With Madame? (She rises.) Never.

CLÉA laughs.

CLÉA

But will there be enough to keep you busy?

ROSE

Busy? Hector needs consolation. He's losing his hair. Francois has warts. And I'm treating Madeleine for shingles.

CLÉA

Good grief Rose, a hospital! You'd be better off coming south with me.

ROSE

(*Quickly, with a big smile*) Oh, Madame! Thank you!

CLÉA

(*Laughs, out-manoeuvred*) Good. We'll eat salade niçoise and play boules in the sun.

ROSE

The bathroom's ready and the electric pads are on the bedside table.

CLÉA

No. Pack it all away. And throw the henna in the sink.

ROSE

(*Shocked*) If you say so, Madame.

She goes.

Left alone, CLÉA stands, scratching herself idly. She crosses to the mirror, inspects her face and the underside of her chin. She stops, thinking she has heard something. But there is silence. She shakes her head, and then sits, head back.

DARLING BOY comes in abruptly. He is pale, out of breath, and looks in a bad mood.

CLÉA

It <u>was</u> you. (*Cool and controlled*) Come in. Hello.

DARLING BOY

Hello. (*More gently*) Hello. (*Slight pause.*) Your light was on.

CLÉA

So, you thought you'd drop in.

DARLING BOY

I've been outside. Are you alone? *(She gestures at the empty room.)* You're not going out?

CLÉA

Not for the moment, no.

DARLING BOY

May I?

She shrugs. He sits down.

DARLING BOY

Are you surprised to see me?

CLÉA

No.

Silence. DARLING BOY gets up and throws off his coat.

CLÉA

Not there. How many times must I tell you. That silk is two hundred years old!

DARLING BOY is looking at her ring. He grabs her hand.

DARLING BOY

What's this?

CLÉA

An emerald.

DARLING BOY

I can see that. Where did you get it?

She does not reply.

DARLING BOY

Who gave it to you?

> CLÉA

Not anyone you know.

> DARLING BOY

Charming.

> CLÉA

It is, isn't it? The colour's wonderful.

> DARLING BOY

I asked you who gave it to you?

> CLÉA

Not your business, wouldn't you say? What are you doing here?

> DARLING BOY

Ah! You mean you're interested?

Silence.

> CLÉA

Have you come to say you're sorry?

> DARLING BOY

Sorry for what?

> CLÉA

That's up to you.

He fidgets restlessly.

> CLÉA

I'm not going to force you.

A long silence.

> DARLING BOY

(*Mutters*) Sorry.

CLÉA

What?

DARLING BOY

(*Louder*) Sorry. (*More gently*) I'm sorry. (*Quickly
retracting it.*) Just to get some peace!

CLÉA

What's upsetting you? Isn't it working out? Don't tell
me she's up to mischief already?

DARLING BOY

Oh, hilarious. (*He laughs, and then turns on her
savagely*) You can cut that out.

CLÉA

'I forbid you to insult my wife.' Isn,t that what you
were going to say?

He starts to kick out at the furniture. She picks up the TELEPHONE.

DARLING BOY

What are you doing?

CLÉA

I'm calling the police.

He pulls the phone away from her.

DARLING BOY

Come on, put it down.

He sits her down, and sits on the floor, leaning against her.

DARLING BOY

You're so cruel. Instead of understanding. Asking
me – decently – what I'm doing here ... (*He goes
quiet.*)

CLÉA

Understanding what?

DARLING BOY

Understanding!

He buries his face in her lap. She bends, takes him in her arms and rocks him gently.

CLÉA

My dear, what's wrong? What have they done to you?

DARLING BOY

Oh, your scent! (*He lifts her pearls, touches her white collar.*) Ohh, it's fantastic. (*He cries and laughs at once.*)

She pulls away, looks at him intently.

CLÉA

(*Softly*) Dear God.

DARLING BOY looks up at her.

CLÉA

Look at me. Why are you here?

DARLING BOY

You know why.

She gazes at him.

DARLING BOY

Have I changed?

CLÉA

You're thinner.

DARLING BOY

I didn't think it would hurt so much.

CLÉA

Oh darling. *(She kisses his face.)* You can't stay.

DARLING BOY

Why not?

CLÉA

You're married.

DARLING BOY

Why didn't you stop me? You should have stopped me!

CLÉA

How could I? Would you have listened?

Silence.

DARLING BOY

I'm coming back.

CLÉA

No, you're not.

DARLING BOY

Yes, I am, I'm here.

CLÉA

Who have you told?

DARLING BOY

Nobody.

CLÉA

Only you and I know?

DARLING BOY

So far. What about you?

CLÉA

What about me?

> DARLING BOY
Are you alone? Is there anyone else?

She looks at him.

> DARLING BOY
There's somebody else.

She does not reply.

> DARLING BOY
You've met someone. Come on, answer me! I'll kick his
face in.

CLÉA laughs, but is near to tears.

> CLÉA
Oh, you idiot. You idiot! Is that what you thought?

> DARLING BOY
So, you don't have a lover.

> CLÉA
No.

> DARLING BOY
You're alone.

> CLÉA
I'm alone.

> DARLING BOY
I knew it.

He sits.

> CLÉA
What did you tell them? Over there.

> DARLING BOY
Let's go to bed.

CLÉA

No, I want to know what sort of mess you've left. Were you hateful?

DARLING BOY

No.

CLÉA

Where is she now?

DARLING BOY

Who?

CLÉA

Your wife!!

DARLING BOY

At Peloux's.

CLÉA

Waiting for you?

DARLING BOY

Perhaps. I don't know.

CLÉA

Have you eaten?

DARLING BOY

Yes, in a bar.

CLÉA

Not at home?

DARLING BOY

I'm home now. (*He gets up and walks round the room, putting out his hand, touching things.*) So this is what they call happiness. I never knew.

He approaches, bends and kisses her hand.

She rises, rings the bell.

ROSE appears.

CLÉA indicates DARLING BOY on the chaise-longue.

> DARLING BOY
>
> Hullo, Rose.

> ROSE
>
> Monsieur. Good evening.

> CLÉA
>
> Rose, in the morning we'll want ...

> ROSE
>
> Lemon tea and sliced melon for Madame, café creme, oeuf au plat et cotelette grillée for Monsieur.

> DARLING BOY
>
> She's a mind-reader.

> CLÉA
>
> Then I'm afraid we shall have to ...

> ROSE
>
> Put back the Chinese room as Monsieur's dressing room?

> CLÉA
>
> If you would.

> DARLING BOY
>
> (To ROSE, points to the valise) What's that?

> ROSE
>
> A valise, M'sieu.

> CLÉA
>
> I was sorting out some things. You can put them away, Rose.

ROSE puts the books and papers back on the desk and leaves with the valise.

The telephone rings.

DARLING BOY jumps up, alert, as she leans over and answers it.

> CLÉA
>
> Hullo … Monsieur who? No, you've got the wrong number, there's no Monsieur here. *(She puts down the telephone.)*

> DARLING BOY
>
> Who was it?

> CLÉA
>
> Wrong number.

DARLING BOY shudders.

> DARLING BOY
>
> I'm cold.

She envelopes him in her arms. They stay, clinging together.

> DARLING BOY
>
> Remember?

> CLÉA
>
> Of course.

> DARLING BOY
>
> I was feeling as I'd always felt in your arms. Safe. Warm …

> CLÉA
>
> It was autumn …

> DARLING BOY
>
> I said …

CLÉA

You said "kiss me."

DARLING BOY

And you went still. So, I kissed you. And you tried to make a joke of it.

CLÉA

And you said . . .

DARLING BOY

I said: "I know all I need to know."

CLÉA

Bloody nerve.

DARLING BOY

You said never mind that. You couldn't see us doing anything. So I made you, and we did. And we went on doing it.

CLÉA

Oh hush.

DARLING BOY

Why? You love me.

CLÉA

Do I?

DARLING BOY

Yes. I was never sure. Until now.

CLÉA

But now you are?

DARLING BOY

Oh yes.

CLÉA

How? Why?

DARLING BOY

Your note.

CLÉA

My note? All I said was goodbye.

DARLING BOY

Exactly.

CLÉA

And that told you I loved you?

DARLING BOY

Oh yes. My wonderful, generous Cléa! Say it. Say you
love me!

They embrace.

Lights down.

ACT TWO – SCENE THREE

Lights up on the same set, early next morning.

The sunlight slants in. The sound of a thrush. Silence, broken by
the sound of the DOORBELL.

ROSE enters, and crosses quickly in a dressing-gown, her greying
hair in a plait.

The sound of VOICES off.

CLÉA enters, tying her elegant negligee, and brushing back her
hair quickly before the mirror as ROSE returns, breathless.

                    ROSE

Madame ...

                    CLÉA

Ssh, he's asleep. What's up?

                    ROSE

A visitor, Madame.

                    CLÉA

At this hour?

                    ROSE

It's Madame Peloux.

                    CLÉA

(*Half asleep*) What the devil does she want? Oh. After
her pedigree pup I suppose ...

CHARLOTTE – hat and hair awry – erupts into the room.

ROSE goes.

                    CLÉA

Charlotte, do come in.

                    CHARLOTTE

Where is he?

                    CLÉA

I'm sorry?

                    CHARLOTTE

Where is he? What have you done with him? Is he
here?

                    CLÉA

Is who here, Charlotte?

                    CHARLOTTE

Darling Boy!!

CLÉA

Darling Boy? Here? Oh, my dear, what's happened?
Oh Charlotte! Not already?

ROSE enters with a tray.

CLÉA pours a brandy for CHARLOTTE who sits, knocks it back
automatically.

CLÉA

Oh, Charlotte . . .

CHARLOTTE

They're asking for the dowry back already.

CLÉA

Well they would.

CHARLOTTE

It's you, isn't it? You've put him up to this. You might
as well admit it. Where have you hidden him? I'm not
leaving till you tell me. Tell me where he is!

CLÉA

Why should I?

CHARLOTTE pursues CLÉA round the room.

CLÉA

Even if I knew . . .

They stand, facing each other.

CHARLOTTE

Oh, I've seen this coming. This started a long time
ago. I had a child and you didn't, so you had to go one
better all the time. Thinner. A bigger establishment.
It's there for all to see. Revenge! It's in your eyes.
It always was. You've been jealous of me since the

old days in the banlieue when my bust put yours to shame. I'm not leaving till you tell me! What are you doing?

CLÉA

(*Picking up bell*) Ringing for help.

CHARLOTTE, with a roar, launches herself at CLÉA, head butts her in the stomach and storms out.

Door slam.

CLÉA thrown back, winded, into an armchair, lifts her head, eyes closed, and laughs quietly.

She jumps as ROSE enters hurriedly.

CLÉA

What is it?

ROSE

Madame Peloux would like a word.

CLÉA

What?! She just tried to kill me!!

The sound of a CAR HOOTING makes her jump.

CLÉA

What's that?

ROSE

It's Madame Peloux's limousine. They're just leaving.

CLÉA

Rose. Will you make sense? If Madame Peloux is leaving, how on earth can she want a word with me?

ROSE

Oh, not Madame Peloux, Madame.

                          CLÉA

Then who?!

                          ROSE

Madame Peloux. Madame Frédéric Peloux. The wife
of ... Monsieur Darling Boy.

                          CLÉA

You mean the little girl? Here?

                          ROSE

Waiting below to see you.

                          CLÉA

No. It's too much. Who let her in?

                          ROSE

Shall I send her away?

                          CLÉA

Yes ... no ... I don't know. What does she want?

                          ROSE

She says it's urgent.

CLÉA groans.

                          CLÉA

Is she upset?

                          ROSE

No, very calm.

                          CLÉA

That sounds ominous.

She walks up and down. ROSE crosses, and pours CLÉA a glass of
Evian. She sips.

                          CLÉA

What does she look like? Is she pretty? Attractive?

ROSE, the good Catholic, cannot lie.

> ROSE

(*Shrugs*) She is young.

> CLÉA

Young. (*Pause*) Oh, send her up.

As ROSE exits, CLÉA quickly sweeps Darling Boy's hat and coat behind the sofa.

ROSE returns, ushers in EDMÉE, then bobs and goes.

> EDMÉE

Madame.

> CLÉA

Madame Peloux, good morning. Might I know to what I owe the privilege? It's very early.

> EDMÉE

No doubt my being here would be a surprise at any hour of the day.

> CLÉA

Not at all.

Hiatus. Neither knows what to say next.

> EDMÉE

I've come about Fred.

> CLÉA

Fred? Oh – yes.

> EDMÉE

It is his name, Madame.

> CLÉA

Yes, well ... What time is it?

EDMÉE

I'm sorry for the inconvenience. Obviously, it's
something serious . . .

CLÉA

(*Panics for a second*) Serious?

EDMÉE

Don't be alarmed. You've nothing to fear from me.

CLÉA

What? Sit down. Please.

EDMÉE

(*Sits*) Fred's gone.

CLÉA

Where?

EDMÉE

I mean he's left me. (*Pause.*) I came to ask if he was
here.

CLÉA

Here? In this house?

EDMÉE

He's not here? But where is he? Where could he be if
he's not . . . ? (*Her voice fails her.*)

CLÉA looks at her without answering.

EDMÉE

I was so sure I'd find him here. I'm sorry. I know I look
ridiculous. We arrived yesterday. I went up to our
room before dinner. When I came down he was gone.

CLÉA

Is that so alarming?

EDMÉE

Yes! I waited and waited. (*A pause*) I know how much
Fred means to you. His fondness for you.

CLÉA

What is your point?

EDMÉE

Obviously, with things as they were, he wouldn't
have come to me without … without your blessing.
(*Bravely*) I've come to ask for him back.

CLÉA

I'm not the one to ask. I've let him go. Now you want
me to get him back for you?

EDMÉE

You're being very unkind.

CLÉA

Unkind? Because I can't do anything for you?

EDMÉE rises, with some dignity.

EDMÉE

Goodbye, Madame.

CLÉA

(*Rises*) You're not going to do something stupid?

EDMÉE

I'm going to look for my husband.

CLÉA

He'll be back. Or he won't. Either way it's for him to
decide.

EDMÉE

No, it isn't.

CLÉA

He'll do as he wants, believe me.

EDMÉE

You make him sound like a monster. If that's what
living here has done, then I'm a lucky escape for him.
He's not yours any more, and not yours to disparage
and criticise and imply that … that …

She stops short.

DARLING BOY has appeared in the doorway. He's in pyjama
bottoms, his hair untidy, his chest bare.

CLÉA, following EDMÉE's gaze, turns and sees him.

DARLING BOY

What's going on?

He advances.

DARLING BOY

This is jolly. What are you doing here? (*Silence.*)
Hmm? (*To CLÉA*) What's she doing here?

CLÉA

What do you think? Kicking up a fuss. Put some
clothes on.

DARLING BOY

(*To EDMÉE*) Why have you … ?

EDMÉE

Don't touch me.

DARLING BOY

I wasn't going to. (*To CLÉA*) Why is she so frightened?
Did you frighten her? (*To EDMÉE*) How did you know
I was here?

CLÉA

Oh, leave the girl alone.

DARLING BOY

Why?

CLÉA

It's over, isn't it?

DARLING BOY

I think that's my business. *(To EDMÉE)* What do you want?

EDMÉE

What do you think I want!

DARLING BOY

You shouldn't be here.

EDMÉE

What about you?!

CLÉA

Oh, for God's sake let her go!

DARLING BOY

(To EDMÉE) Why come here? You should have waited.

EDMÉE

Waited? For what?

DARLING BOY

Go home and wait for me.

EDMÉE

For what?

DARLING BOY

For whatever I decide.

She looks at him, and goes. He crosses to the window and looks
down to see her go. The door closes, offstage.

> CLÉA
>
> I'm sorry. It's my fault. I should never have let her in.
> But I was afraid she'd start making a fuss and wake
> the whole household.

He doesn't answer.

> CLÉA
>
> You were wonderful. So, adult. You usually react like
> a twelve-year-old.

> DARLING BOY
>
> Hard not to, with you.

CLÉA flinches, but rallies.

> CLÉA
>
> It's the secret of your charm. Just now when you were
> talking, I could hear myself. I thought: he's got it from
> me, that authority.

> DARLING BOY
>
> You sound surprised.

> CLÉA
>
> I'm flattered. Though it makes me wonder what
> you're here for.

> DARLING BOY
>
> I'm here for help.

> CLÉA
>
> Help? Why?

DARLING BOY

Because it's not possible to change everything overnight. How am I to manage? I don't know what to do. How am I supposed to cope with all this? I need you to tell me. You're my window on the world.

CLÉA collapses in tears.

CLÉA

Oh, you are so, so selfish! No, no more words. It's better to keep quiet before … (*She weeps quietly*). You didn't tell me she was beautiful.

He kisses her hands gently.

DARLING BOY

My Cléa … My poor Cléa …

CLÉA, furious, snatches her hands away.

CLÉA

Stop it! Stop that. "Poor Cléa"! Did I come looking for you?D'you think I don't know what you're up to? Here tonight, there tomorrow, here the night after? How long d'you think that'll last before she … That girl's mother is Marie-Louise! Like mother, like daughter.

DARLING BOY

Cléa!

CLÉA

Don't think you can bully me like you can that child.

DARLING BOY

Stop it.

CLÉA

No, I won't stop it.

DARLING BOY

Yes, you will. You are not going to spoil everything. I
won't let you spoil my Cléa ...

CLÉA

(Pulls away) Don't ...

DARLING BOY

Is that how Cléa would talk? My Cléa, who showed me
that she loved me by sending me a note, letting me go.
To make me happy. (He kisses her gently.) Remember
what you said to me just before the wedding?

CLÉA

I don't remember saying anything.

DARLING BOY

No, you were very quiet. But you did tell me. What did
you tell me?

CLÉA

Not to be mean.

DARLING BOY

Not to let her suffer. That's Cléa! Even in there
(He nods his head towards the bedroom) you were
worried about how much harm we were doing.
Hurting someone weaker than ...

CLÉA

No, stronger! Happier! The one you're going back to.

Silence.

CLÉA

Why did you come? Why did you make love to me?
Without that, I could have managed.

DARLING BOY

I needed my warm, safe place. Cléa, was it worse to do
what we did than sit side by side on a sofa talking all
night? I don't think so.

CLÉA

If only you hadn't stayed.

DARLING BOY

I came because I needed you. I needed to see you.

CLÉA

You needed. It's always <u>you</u>, isn't it?

DARLING BOY

Yes! Me! Here I am, drunk as ever on the happiness
of what we do together – of what you give me. But you
saw her. How frightened she is!

CLÉA

Of course she's frightened. Her happiness, and her
whole life, now depend on you.

DARLING BOY

Me?

CLÉA

How do you feel about that?

DARLING BOY

(Thinks) It's a worry.

CLÉA

I daresay. Not what you've done before, is it? Take
care of someone. Do you love her?

DARLING BOY

No. That's another worry. How can I tell her I love her
when I don't? How can I lie to her?

CLÉA

Of course you can lie to her.

DARLING BOY

You want me to?

CLÉA

Yes! Until you accept that you do love her.

DARLING BOY

I do?

CLÉA

Would you have married her otherwise? Done
something you didn't want to do? Darling Boy! We
both know better than that.

DARLING BOY

Do we?

CLÉA

I'm over. It's her turn to tremble.

They stand, gazing at each other.

CLÉA

Time for you to go.

DARLING BOY

I don't want to go.

CLÉA

Whether you do or not! You must see. It might as well
be now as later.

He stares at her without answering.

DARLING BOY

I don't know what to do.

                    CLÉA

Do as I tell you. Go home.

                 DARLING BOY

    Home!

                    CLÉA

Get dressed. (*As he turns obediently*) No! Don't go
back in there! I'll get your things.

She goes, and returns at once with his clothes.

He is standing by the window, his body shining in the dazzling
sunlight. She catches her breath.

He turns. She hands him his clothes and watches as he dresses.
He puts on a shoe, then hops, looking for the other. She points to it
and he puts it on.

                    CLÉA

    Off you go.

But he cannot go. He looks at her. Then shakes his head.

                    CLÉA

    (*Quietly*) Darling Boy ... do as I say.

He tries to approach her, but she steps back and waves him away.
Furious and stricken, he looks at her, then turns and goes quickly.

CLÉA stands still. Then, forcing herself to move, she walks about,
fetching up in front of the looking glass. She inspects her face,
touches her jawline.

Lost, she moves about, tidying absently.

                    CLÉA

    Why?

She moves back and forth, distracted.

CLÉA

Settle for what you can get! Call him back! He'll come.
No. Don't do that. No. No.

The DOORBELL rings.

CLÉA

(*Turns*) Darling Boy?

She goes to the window.

Fade to black.

The End

CEDRIC & LOUISE

FOREWORD

CEDRIC & LOUISE was Pam Gems's last full-length play. She wrote it in 2010, when she was eighty-five.

Printed here is the second draft, which may be unfinished as she never did less than six drafts of anything. She liked to say: "A play isn't written, it's rewritten and rewritten and rewritten and rewritten."

For example, she did eighteen drafts of QUEEN CHRISTINA – and two post-production drafts after that.

Unfinished or not, CEDRIC & LOUISE is an interesting piece, which touches lightly on a range of issues, and looks at death in a clear-eyed, non-sentimental way that is quintessentially Pam.

The incident of the school Literary Prize happened, almost exactly as described, when Pam was a fifteen-year-old pupil at Brockenhurst Grammar school in Hampshire.

In many ways, LOUISE resembles her younger self. Like Louise, Pam, was from a poor background with two brothers and no father. CEDRIC might be, in part, her older self – an ailing oldster (as Pam was when she wrote it) at the end of a lifetime of significant work, who concludes that, ultimately: "We don't know anything."

Jonathan Gems
January 2022

CEDRIC & LOUISE

CHARACTERS

CEDRIC – An aging scientist

LOUISE – A student

CEDRIC & LOUISE

<u>SCENE ONE</u>

Cedric's Study.

CEDRIC – elderly – is reading in an easy chair by a table laden with books and papers.

Across the room, on the floor, a teenage girl, LOUISE, lies on her stomach reading *Paris Match* magazine. She turns a page.

CEDRIC turns a page.

> LOUISE
>
> *(Reaching for a biscuit tin)* Rich Tea or Ginger?

He holds out a hand without raising his eyes from the page. She swims across the carpet, and puts a biscuit in his hand. He eats without looking up. She snakes back, finds her place and resumes reading on her stomach. He reaches for a pen, and makes a brief note.

> LOUISE
>
> Sortable! *(French pronunciation.)*

CEDRIC lifts his head. She reaches for a dictionary on the floor.

> LOUISE
>
> *(To herself)* Sortable.

> CEDRIC
>
> *(Calls)* Presentable.

She flips the pages, finds the word, and nods.

> CEDRIC
>
> 'Pas sortable' means you can't be seen out with him.

She chuckles. They both continue working.

LOUISE

Essayeur? (*Looks in the dictionary*) essayeur . . .
essayeuse . . .

CEDRIC

Means fitter. As in tailoring.

LOUISE

Don't think so.

She gets up, and brings him her copy of *Paris Match*. He looks
where she points, reads and laughs.

CEDRIC

(*Looking up at her*) Here it means a woman being
tried out as a high-class escort.

LOUISE

(*Leaning for a look*) What, a tart you mean?

CEDRIC

That's what the scandal's about. He's been rumbled.
There's the white flag (*Points at the page.*) Wife
clamped to his side with a fixed smile.

LOUISE

Oh.

CEDRIC turns the magazine pages to look at the pictures.

LOUISE

Will he lose his job?

CEDRIC

No. Whoever shopped him will be moved sideways.

LOUISE

For being a snitch?

CEDRIC

For being bourgeois. C'est pas sortable.

LOUISE chuckles, and jolts him on the shoulder as he turns a page.

LOUISE

Hold on. Turn back. (*Takes the magazine from him.*)

CEDRIC

What?

LOUISE

(*Points*) Agynesse Dehn. English model. (*Excited*)
Kate Moss!

CEDRIC

(*Looking*) Mmm?

LOUISE

Only the topmost model in the world. Emblems of the
era – that's what Sparky calls them.

He looks puzzled.

LOUISE

(*To herself*) Jesus! (*Aloud*) Sparky says if you wanna
know about history look at the visuals.

CEDRIC

Who's Sparky?

LOUISE

Art teacher. (*Turns a page. Stabs at a picture.*) Tam
Johnson. He's the latest male model. There are some
cool older guys modelling now. So long as they're not
bald. Shaved head's okay.

CEDRIC

Any older women models?

LOUISE

No. Maybe in France. Older women in France are chic.

CEDRIC

I'll call my travel agent.

She smiles briefly, and turns the pages.

LOUISE

(Without lifting her head) Did you go to the hospital?

CEDRIC

Yup.

LOUISE

Okay?

CEDRIC

Next appointment in six months.

LOUISE

You have to go back?

CEDRIC

With prostate, once you've got it, what's important is
the rate of advance.

LOUISE

What's yours?

CEDRIC

Not galloping.

She yocks with laughter. He looks up.

LOUISE

Sorry. *(Slight pause.)* What if it does decide to gallop?

CEDRIC

They give you drugs.

CEDRIC

Any good?

CEDRIC

Yup.

LOUISE

What does Ruby say?

CEDRIC

(*Foreign accent*) "Dos, you are lost."

LOUISE

Dos?

CEDRIC

Means 'friend' in Kazakh.

LOUISE

In other words, 'You've had it, mate.' Ruby's scared of getting deported.

CEDRIC

I know. (*Shakes his head.*) I keep telling her. As my wife . . .

LOUISE

She'll still anxious though. If you fall under a bus, she'll have to find some other mug. (*Settles down with her magazine.*) Why did you marry her? I don't know why you did that.

CEDRIC

So she wouldn't be deported.

LOUISE

Yeah, but now you've lumbered yourself. (*She flicks him a look of admiration for his gallantry.*) What you should do is demand your marital rights. That would scare her off.

CEDRIC

Don't talk nonsense.

LOUISE

Actually, she'd probably be grateful. What with that moustache.

CEDRIC

Highly prized in Kazakhstan. Sign of a fertile woman. A bearded virgin will get a husband with no dowry.

LOUISE

(*Jumps up.*) I need to go to Tesco's. Do you need anything?

CEDRIC

No. What are you cooking your brothers tonight?

LOUISE

Leftovers and stewed apple.

CEDRIC

(*He fishes in his pocket, and hands her some money.*) Here.

LOUISE

Thanks!

CEDRIC

They're growing lads.

She laughs, happy with gratitude, and dashes off.

He bends to his work.

Fade to black.

<u>SCENE TWO</u>

Cedric's Garden.

A stylish paved area with seating and pots, hedging, and trees
beyond.

CEDRIC and the LOUISE enjoy the sun. He has taken off his jacket,
and lies back, eyes closed. She throws crumbs to the birds.

CEDRIC

(*Murmurs*) You'll encourage the pigeons.

LOUISE

Don't be mean. Share the planet.

CEDRIC

Who says?

LOUISE

Eco-Alliance.

CEDRIC

What's that?

LOUISE

It's on Facebook.

CEDRIC

Ah!

She throws crumbs for the birds.

She nudges him gently as a ROBIN approaches. They watch, and lift
their heads together, to see the birds fly off.

CEDRIC

Robin. Mr Solo. A loner. Except when mating.
Tough little bird. (*Slight pause.*) I had a rat once. I
was marking papers in my rooms at Oxford, and it

ran over my foot. Damnedest thing. It stood there considering its options, which weren't great. Looked up at me, strolled back over my shoe, and buggered off. I should have clobbered it.

LOUISE

But you didn't?

CEDRIC

No. We lived together for about a year. It's always humbling: courage in adversity.

LOUISE

(She thinks.) Depends what you've got courage for. It could have been a lady rat with babies to protect.

They settle back and relax in the sun.

LOUISE

I wonder if it's true for non-mammals.

CEDRIC

What?

LOUISE

Mother-love. Do all species care for their young?

CEDRIC

Shouldn't think so. Most of them are more like components. Which doesn't stop them stinging you.

LOUISE

Aphids don't bite.

CEDRIC

No, too busy guzzling. You should see my beans.

LOUISE

They've got to eat something.

CEDRIC

Why my beans?

LOUISE

Well, they don't realise. Unlike Uncle Norman, my
father's brother.

CEDRIC

Ate his beans, did they?

LOUISE

No, he conned my Dad out of his share of the family
home. We really needed the money. If it weren't for
that, Dad might not have left.

CEDRIC

Yes. *(Slight pause.)* Families don't always work. Still
the best idea though.

LOUISE

Think so?

CEDRIC

In the end, yes. Too much freedom leads to
bewilderment. You see it in children. Without
parameters, they don't know who they are.

LOUISE

People get together when things go wrong. Otherwise,
it's take care of yourself.

CEDRIC

Teachers, doctors, dentists …

LOUISE

(Cutting him off) That's just maintenance. I'm
talking about who's in charge.

CEDRIC

And who's that?

LOUISE

Me!

CEDRIC

(Laughs) If you say so.

LOUISE

I do.

CEDRIC

What about the unfortunate? The people who need help? Are you saying … (Index finger across his throat with a harsh hiss) kkkkk!

LOUISE

Yes. Serve them right.

CEDRIC

For what?

LOUISE

For being stupid. For living in a fantasy world.

CEDRIC

Oh, come on! Even Einstein said the most important element in a successful life was luck. Some people thrive – for others it's heads below the parapet.

LOUISE

Everyone's different. Everyone's unique. That means you. You decide.

CEDRIC

A matter of options.

LOUISE

Yeah. You figure things out. Figure the odds. Toe in
the water. Take the plunge!

CEDRIC

And caveat emptor.

LOUISE

What does that mean?

CEDRIC

It's Latin for 'watch it, buster.'

LOUISE

Yeah, that as well.

He smiles, lies back, relaxing, and starts to tap his fingers on his
chest.

LOUISE

What?

CEDRIC

Oh nothing. Just … Perhaps an atavistic moment of
yearning for something else. Something poetic. I'm
being romantic. What do I know? Totally unreliable.

LOUISE

What?

CEDRIC

Oh … feeling.

LOUISE

Feeling?

CEDRIC

Feelings. Why do we still believe ... ? Why these obstinate attachments to notions of – of – (*throws up his hands, looking for the word.*)

LOUISE

Of what?

CEDRIC

Gallantry. The moment. Rising to the occasion. Complete bloody waste of time.

LOUISE

I don't see why. If somebody does something special ...

CEDRIC

But you can't rely ... you can't depend on, or guarantee, the moment.

LOUISE

Why not?

CEDRIC

It's not necessarily there, quantifiable – available on demand.

LOUISE

Sure it is. In some people. Some people are naturally brave – or naturally timid. Probably runs in families.

CEDRIC

No. Take my word for it. Response to crisis – accident – never stable. Human beings have many qualities. Predictable, reliable responses to stimuli – (*Shakes his head.*) No. It's why you have to hard-train soldiers.

LOUISE

To get them to fight.

CEDRIC

There again you never know. Though it's easier than you might suppose.

LOUISE

Well boys like fighting. Girls like dolls. Boys like swords and guns.

CEDRIC

And looting. And raping.

LOUISE

Most people …

CEDRIC

Most people are capable of anything – for self-preservation. Absolutely anything.

LOUISE

So, if I fall in, and Peter – you haven't met him – jumps in after me, I should tell him to fuck off, quit being a romantic prat, just let me get caught in the weeds and drown.

CEDRIC

Now you're being silly.

LOUISE

No, I'm not.

CEDRIC

Yes, you are, you want a fight.

LOUISE

So do you.

A pause. He stirs at last.

> LOUISE

What?

He shakes his head, makes to subside, changes his mind.

> CEDRIC

When you're young, you feel immortal. And that can be exploited. It doesn't last. Gone by your twenties. Sooner in battle. If you do dodge the Reaper, it's no more dreams of victory. It's how the hell do I survive? If being brave looks like doing you in ...

LOUISE laughs.

> LOUISE

Who wants to be a dead hero!

> CEDRIC

Exactly. Glad, you agree.

A pause. He smiles to himself.

> LOUISE

What?

> CEDRIC

Oh nothing.

> LOUISE

What?

> CEDRIC

We had this little ginger, pink-eyed chap in the pay office. Never opened his mouth except to say sorry.

He stops. She waits.

CEDRIC

We were crossing this paddy field after a fairly rough morning. No cover. Much too quiet. All of a sudden, Ginger streak takes off – sprints over the ground, full-tossing hand grenades to extra cover, square leg, like an England team fast bowler. Took out a whole bunker. Amazing.

LOUISE

Was he killed?

CEDRIC

No. Probably because he was five foot nothing. Dodgy target. When I asked him what the hell he thought he was doing, he apologised. He said the flies had been driving him up the wall, and would I overlook it?

LOUISE

Wow. Did they give him a medal?

CEDRIC

They would have if he hadn't stepped on a mine.

Pause.

LOUISE

Were you brave? In Korea?

CEDRIC

Of course not. Wars of futility promote highly sophisticated modes of self-preservation.

LOUISE

So, you weren't brave then?

CEDRIC

Only occasionally.

LOUISE

(*Eager*) Where?

CEDRIC

In the boxing ring, usually.

LOUISE

You were a boxer?

CEDRIC

Amateur. Light-middle-weight.

LOUISE

Did you win?

CEDRIC

Sometimes. Before the fight began.

LOUISE

You mean because they were fixed?

CEDRIC

No. You look in their eyes.

LOUISE

Your opponents? And that tells you? (*She nods, digesting this.*) Did you enjoy it?

CEDRIC

Boxing? Yes. Didn't realise it at the time. You don't.

LOUISE

Happy? To punch people?

CEDRIC

Yes.

LOUISE

You could have got brain damage. Probably did.

                    CEDRIC
Worth it for the bliss.

                    LOUISE
Bliss?

                    CEDRIC
Yes ... a rare state. You see it in dogs sometimes.
Babies. Young strikers after scoring – before they've
learned to cool it.

                    LOUISE
Strikers go berserk.

                    CEDRIC
That's triumphalism. Not the same as joy.

He picks up his jacket from the back of the bench.

                    LOUISE
(As they exit) Joy?

                                        Fade to black.

SCENE THREE

A Café.

CEDRIC and the LOUISE are having coffee. She stirs her cup,
frowning.

                    LOUISE
Not my favourite word, joy. *(She leans across the
table towards him.)* Her Christian name.

                    CEDRIC
(Taking a roll and butter.) Madam Miasma?

LOUISE

How did you know?

CEDRIC

The whiff of sulphur.

LOUISE

We try to avoid her. Janey Ironside said to her once:
"Sorry, Miss Harper, could I have some water, please?
You're making me feel faint."

CEDRIC

(*Buttering his roll*) How was that received?

She looks at him scornfully.

LOUISE

(*Mincing voice*) "I don't know why you girls are so in
awe of me – I'm just a human being, you know."

He laughs.

LOUISE

Caught me this morning. "Could I borrow you?" I
was in the library, and she saw me. She beckoned me
across the hall to her door. (*She groans heavily.*) Her
study. Abandon Hope, all ye who enter here.

He chuckles.

CEDRIC

Intimidating?

LOUISE

Worse.

He smiles at her gloomy expression, and stirs his coffee.

CEDRIC

(*Thoughtful*) "If you want to know the secrets of me
you must first learn the real me."

She looks at him, frowning in puzzlement.

CEDRIC

Imagination. Has to be there. Not dried out and
shoved on top of the wardrobe, like most people's.
Locate the imagination. Locate it and invade it.

LOUISE

Imagination? From Madam 'You Can Always Rely on
Harrods?' (*She shakes her head.*) We're talking about
the Iron Age. The Carboniferous Layer.

Pause.

CEDRIC

What did she want to see you about?

LOUISE

You.

CEDRIC

Me?

LOUISE

She's after you again. Could you be persuaded to
grace us with your presence? She even uncapped the
Mont Blanc. Got out the Diary. Oh God.

He gives her a tender look, unseen.

CEDRIC

What did you say?

CEDRIC & LOUISE

LOUISE

I said you had the clap, stage Two. And weeping
ulcers.

CEDRIC reacts.

LOUISE

I'm joking. I said you work all the time. <u>All</u> the time.
And I'm the reason you stop sometimes, because I
take your mind off.

CEDRIC

Don't put yourself down.

LOUISE

It's true. Partly. Sometimes. Mostly, you aren't
listening.

CEDRIC

Of course, I listen.

LOUISE

Liar. Well, occasionally.

He regards her.

LOUISE

What?

CEDRIC

You remind me of something ... probably of when
there was time for a me.

She pulls a face at him, puzzled.

CEDRIC

It's the price you pay. There's always a price.

She looks away, baffled, as she often is with him.

                    CEDRIC

So, you put her off?

                    LOUISE

I did. Actually, I was rather subtle.

                    CEDRIC

(*Laughs*) Subtle?

                    LOUISE

I said that, although this was not known to the
general public, the reason for your rare appearances
on the platform was due to – guess.

He drinks his coffee. She leans across the table.

                    LOUISE

Your handicap. A burden born bravely since early
childhood.

                    CEDRIC

Not the clap then?

                    LOUISE

No. (*Offers him more cake.*) An infirmity known only
to members of your inner family – and, of course, Her
Majesty. The reason you didn't show up in Oslo. What
disability would stop you from taking your place as a
major star in the scientific firmament?

                    CEDRIC

I give up.

                    LOUISE

Give up?

                    CEDRIC

I've just said so.

She leans across, and grasps his hand in pity.

LOUISE

Your stammer.

CEDRIC absorbs this. Nods.

LOUISE

You can't deal with the letter P.

CEDRIC

P?

LOUISE

P. I said that, one day, you were so despairing, you
asked for my help.

CEDRIC

What did I want?

LOUISE

You said ... You apologised but urgently needed, for
your work, to know how many p's ... (*She pauses*) You
wanted to know how many p's there were in p-p-p-p-
pepper ... was it five or six?

He throws a cake at her. It hits her and falls on the floor. She picks
it up.

LOUISE

No, I said your calendar was filled up for the next
two years. I said you were going to Paris and Zurich
and Beijing, but she mustn't tell anyone, 'cause it was
classified. She was round that desk like a ferret on
uppers. I had to bat her away!

CEDRIC

Hm!

> LOUISE

She said I was not to worry. She said I was a credit to the school. She said if I ever need to talk to someone, I could knock on her door anytime. You have your uses, you old sod.

He laughs.

> LOUISE

And Mrs Jenkins stopped me in the corridor this morning. She told me my essay on deserts was a hit in the staff room. They're all suddenly being nice to me. I don't like it.

> CEDRIC

Deserts?

> LOUISE

Yeah.

> CEDRIC

You've never seen a desert.

> LOUISE

So?

> CEDRIC

If you'd had one term of elementary science in that phony showplace of yours – and I don't mean computers.

> LOUISE

Oh, not that again.

> CEDRIC

(*Irritable*) What the hell do you know about deserts?

LOUISE

Listen. As a student of the arts, I have an imagination fed by books and movies. I don't need the dehydrated aridities of science. I'm a gifted, romantic intellectual. At least, I will be.

CEDRIC

Which thrives without need of science.

LOUISE

I did chemistry for a term! Bloody boring. Thank God it was optional.

CEDRIC

And dispensable.

LOUISE

I didn't say that. Of course we need science. For things like nuclear fission ... and cosmetics.

She giggles.

He looks at her amiably.

CEDRIC

(Dreamily) And the Second Law?

LOUISE

Law?

CEDRIC

Of thermo-dynamics

She looks at him with defensive wariness.

CEDRIC

Let me demonstrate. (He puts a book on end, and knocks it over.) Can you reverse that?

LOUISE

Yeah, easy. (*Picks up the book and puts it back on the café table.*)

CEDRIC

No, I said reverse. You have created a subsequent occurrence. The Second Law of Thermo-dynamics expresses the fact that things happen one way. An awesome realisation, as no doubt you are aware.

LOUISE

(*Defensive*) I don't think so, no.

CEDRIC

Of course not, how could you? You're not equipped to know, nor to experience the celestial intoxication of realising that two and two do not, necessarily, make four. You, my young sprout, are a Neanderthal.

LOUISE

Neanderthal? Because I can be moved by the nothingness of space? By air unimpeded by moisture? Light unmolested by cloud? What's wrong with deserts?

CEDRIC

Nothing.

LOUISE

Then what are you on about?

CEDRIC

Idiotic tendencies in humans.

LOUISE

What is wrong with deserts? Shortage of facilities? No on-street parking, chicken takeaways, or all night pharmacies?

CEDRIC

Although the drawbacks of deserts – vegetatively,
habitationally and culturally – are widely known,
their more profound danger . . .

LOUISE

Deserts aren't dangerous.

CEDRIC

I disagree.

LOUISE

No more than anything else.

CEDRIC

Of course. Benevolent or the reverse, depending on
the wisdom or derangement of human involvement . . .
degree of romantic idiocy.

LOUISE

A can of Red Bull, and no sunhat, for a walk across
the Sahara, for example . . .

CEDRIC

I was thinking of another sort of risk.

LOUISE

What?

CEDRIC

Tendencies capable of inciting conditions leading
to . . . to trauma.

LOUISE

Trauma? I'm talking about deserts. What are you
talking about? Prickly heat?

CEDRIC

(*Shakes his head*) No, another sort of trauma. I
suppose you could call it Trauma Lawrentius.

LOUISE

Trauma Lawrentius?

CEDRIC

Yes. Lawrentius. Lawrence T.E.

LOUISE

You mean Lawrence of Arabia?

She rises, and looms over him.

LOUISE

Just because I like deserts doesn't mean I'm a
repressed gay who craves welts on his bum.

He looks round to see if they are being overheard.

LOUISE

T. E. Lawrence was a great big middle-class phony.

CEDRIC

Who lived at the daily risk of being shoved in the
clink for being a queer. That's how it was for us dated
old has-beens.

LOUISE

Yeah, yeah, and women were strung up as witches.
Anyway, you're not gay.

CEDRIC

No, though at times it would seem to offer the better
option, all things considered. (*Pause.*) So – you got it.
The Literary Prize.

LOUISE

Yup.

CEDRIC

I wondered why you were looking so ...

LOUISE

Like the cat that got the cream?

CEDRIC

I was going to say in such a good mood.

LOUISE

(*Laughs*) Yeah. Got it. 'Enfin my dear knight.' I must
stop doing that.

CEDRIC

Doing what?

LOUISE

Quoting. Doesn't go down well.

CEDRIC

Why not?

LOUISE

Marks you out as a reader.

CEDRIC

That's not good?

LOUISE

Absolument pas. Fuck, I've done it again.

CEDRIC

Reading not cool?

LOUISE

No. Very last century. Like VHS tapes.

He digests this with deep dismay. Which she notices.

LOUISE

There'll always be a minority, like liken – or is it pronounced lichen – on the trees. A few quaint souls who don't rely on smart-phones. I'm thinking of starting a new secret society of neo-primitives called the Neeps.

CEDRIC

The Neeps?

LOUISE

(*Nods*) Neo-primitives.

CEDRIC

Would there be many of you? Enough for a decent-sized movement?

LOUISE

I wouldn't bet on it.

CEDRIC

I'm surprised they still have prizes in that school of yours. Don't they find it racist or something?

LOUISE

Well, they didn't want to give it to me because of my unreasonable behaviour.

CEDRIC

A decent degree of deference.

LOUISE

More about not wearing nose rings, tattoos, or jeans showing your bum-crack. Plus – what you said.

CEDRIC

Hardly your style, deference. Your father should have been court-martialed. Completely buggered up the line of command.

LOUISE

(*Remembers, smiling*) He sent me some money!

CEDRIC

Your father? Bravo, how much?

LOUISE

A lot. He must have had a good day at Epsom. I got a Westwood jacket and Louboutin heels. Four inch. I tried the six inch but I fell over.

He smiles with polite sympathy.

CEDRIC

What do you get for your prize?

LOUISE

A book. What do you think?

CEDRIC

Who chooses?

LOUISE

Me.

CEDRIC

Oh.

LOUISE

Don't start. You're allowed to leave out Shakespeare, wouldn't you know. But you're supposed to pick some worthy tome. So it looks good on the platform.

CEDRIC

How much do they spend on it?

LOUISE

Fifty, sixty – maybe more.

CEDRIC

Sixty quid? (*Thoughtful, to himself.*) Hmmm.

Pause.

LOUISE

I don't want some fucking doorstop.

CEDRIC

I'm thinking.

LOUISE

Year before last, Madeleine Annetts got away with buying a Roger Hilton book. That cost about sixty. Lovely rickety drawings of women's fannies.

CEDRIC

Get *The Feynman Lectures on Physics* by Richard Feynman. It covers basic physics. Electromagnetism. All the way up to quantum mechanics.

She makes a face.

CEDRIC

No, you'll enjoy it. He's funny. He once played bongos for the San Francisco ballet.

LOUISE

I'll ask for paperbacks. You can get more books that way. I'll ask for a hundred-quid's worth.

They look at each other.

Fade to black.

SCENE FOUR

The Study.

LOUISE and CEDRIC sit across from each other at the round table, illuminated by a table lamp. She has pen and paper. He nods for her to read out the list in front of her.

> LOUISE
> (*Reads*) Conrad, James, Wharton, Wodehouse,
> Simenon, Elmore Leonard, early Amis M ... Blow
> the lot on Proust? (*Looks up*) In French? (*Shakes
> her head.*) Saul Bellow ... Tennyson – best ear in the
> business – Larkin, Beckett ...

> CEDRIC
> Too many, d'you think?

> LOUISE
> Wow. It takes a rarified scientific genius to figure
> that out.

> CEDRIC
> Come on. How many shall we say? Thirty?

> LOUISE
> (*Shakes her head*) No chance.

> CEDRIC
> Twenty.

> LOUISE
> Paperbacks don't cost 50p. Maybe in your day.

> CEDRIC
> One and sixpence.

She looks baffled.

                    CEDRIC

Fifteen pence.

                    LOUISE

(Amazed) What!

                    CEDRIC

It was worth more then. How many do you want?

She shrugs.

                    CEDRIC

Look, I'll buy the rest for you.

No response.

                    CEDRIC

What's wrong with that?

                    LOUISE

Okay, if you must.

He holds out his hand for the list. She gives it to him. He reads it.

                    CEDRIC

Fine. Submit it.

She shakes her head.

                    CEDRIC

Why not?

                    LOUISE

What's the point? They'll either think I've gone daft
or I'll get sworn at. Either way that'll be the end of it.

                    CEDRIC

They can't just dismiss the whole thing out of ...

CEDRIC & LOUISE
LOUISE

If I was up for the percussion prize, that's a trip for the winners to Buenos Aires for the International Jazz Fest.

CEDRIC

(Waves her down) Learn to stand your ground. If you want books – never mind whether reading's in fashion or not – show the list to Mrs Jenkins. Make your case. Go for it.

LOUISE

(Flat) Okay.

She grabs her satchel and moves off without enthusiasm.

She pauses at the exit. He looks at her in enquiry.

CEDRIC

Now what?

LOUISE

Just in case you had a better idea.

He laughs, and waves her off.

She looks at him, dispirited, and goes.

He drops the cheerfulness and looks after her thoughtfully.

Fade to black.

SCENE FIVE

A Hospital Ward.

CEDRIC is propped up in bed, reading.

Pause.

The peace is disturbed by the LOUISE entering noisily. He looks up over his glasses as she approaches and upends her cloth carrier bag on the bed.

> **LOUISE**
> New toothbrush, biros, whisky, and claret and sod fucking Nurse Big-arse who keeps breathing all over you.

He watches as she fills his locker.

> **CEDRIC**
> Very cool hands. I may marry her.

> **LOUISE**
> You'd be dead in six months. She'd be at the poison cabinet for your bank balance.

> **CEDRIC**
> Ah, but in between . . .

She stands over him, brandishing chocolate and a bottle of wine.

> **LOUISE**
> Chocolate with nuts and ginger.

> **CEDRIC**
> (*Pointing to the wine.*) Some of that I think.

She grins, produces a corkscrew from her pocket, tries to open the bottle, but gives up, and hands it to him.

> **LOUISE**
> Are you still . . . ?

> **CEDRIC**
> No. Feeling more myself. As they say.

She looks at him, and nods sceptically.

CEDRIC

I have, however, after taking advice, abandoned
cycling.

He opens the bottle as she finds a glass and a teacup.

LOUISE

(*Rises*) Yes … well … being knocked down not once,
twice, three times, four times, but five times, has to
be some sort of a hint, don't you think?

He pours. They drink. She sits on the bed.

LOUISE

You're too old for cycling.

CEDRIC

Einstein cycled when he was ninety – ninety-one.

He lies back and closes his eyes.

LOUISE

What is it with you?

CEDRIC

As the great Ronaldinho says: "I am ugly, but I have
charm."

LOUISE

Don't change the subject.

He opens his eyes.

LOUISE

It's the way you fade out. Bleach the canvas. Turn
into a ghost. Everybody else joins the human race.
Why not you? What is it? Swank?

CEDRIC

(Taken off balance.) Swank? I don't think so. I hope not.

LOUISE

(Peruses him.) You should see my tits. They're like something by Botticelli. Nobody ever sees them except me. *(She lifts her t-shirt.)*

CEDRIC

(Genuine obeisance) Thank you. They're lovely.

LOUISE

No-one's ever seen them. Apart from you now. I should be sleeping with Ralph Fiennes. He lives down the road from us.

CEDRIC

He pronounces it Rafe.

LOUISE

How would you know? You don't watch films. You don't see anything. I'm your only visitor, and you only put up with me because I don't matter.

She offers him chocolates. He shakes his head. She bends, choosing one. He gazes at her tenderly.

LOUISE

Are you still on the morphine?

CEDRIC

Nope.

LOUISE

Good. *(Sitting in the chair by the bed.)* You missed a treat. Founder's Day Festival. I did my crazy-dance.

She jumps up and dances.

He applauds.

She throws herself on her back at the bottom of the bed.

CEDRIC

LOUISE

I'm free!

CEDRIC

Bravissimo.

She sits up and they smile at each other.

CEDRIC

(*Quietly*) So, what now?

She jumps down, evading the question. Then turns to him.

LOUISE

I got the books.

She looks gloomy and grinds her teeth.

CEDRIC

What went wrong?

LOUISE

Wrong?

CEDRIC

Don't grind your teeth. With the books.

LOUISE

Nothing. (*Silence.*) I thought the best thing was to show the list to Mrs Jenkins. Ask her to take it to Madame la Directrice – aka Miasma Ode-to-Joy-Not.

CEDRIC

What did she say – Jenkins . . . ?

LOUISE

She looked at the list, handed it back, and said I must take it myself.

CEDRIC

Backed off?

LOUISE

(Shrugs) Dunno. Anyway, I took it over to Abandon Hope during break. I was going to leave it with the secretary. I didn't think Miasma would be there.

CEDRIC

But she was.

LOUISE

Yah. Sitting by the window, drinking coffee.

CEDRIC

All okay?

LOUISE

(Guarded, after a slight pause) I got the big smile. Congratulations. Interested to hear my choice of book.

He waits.

LOUISE

(Absently) She didn't ask me to sit down. *(Comes to)* I handed her the list. And there was this wonderful silence. Just the sound of the tennis.

CEDRIC

What did she say?

LOUISE

(Turns to him suddenly) I wish you'd been there. Give Miasma her due, she can lay it on. Her best thing.

Her only thing really. She got up and went behind her desk, dangling the list across it. Waving it in my face fast enough to make you boss-eyed. I realised something was up when somebody knocked on the door and she yapped at them to go away.

CEDRIC

(*Posh*) Go away!

LOUISE

(*Mean shriek*) "Go Away!" I just stood there. Anyway, she put the list down and asked if this was my idea of a joke.

CEDRIC

A joke? What did you say?

LOUISE

I said the cost of seven softbacks was no more than one quality hardback. She said that wasn't the point. I said I was sorry, but what did she mean? Something like that. She said ... she said ... (*Her voice breaks slightly*) She said no doubt I wasn't aware of the enormity and unacceptability of what I'd done.

CEDRIC

Which was?

LOUISE

(*Hardening*) Apparently, I was being exploitative. I was misusing an occasion designed to celebrate achievement, to exploit the staff and fellow pupils, and the school, and what it stood for.

He hoists himself up in fury.

CEDRIC

(*Mutters*) Bitch.

LOUISE

I know. I said I didn't understand. What I was
supposed to have done? Which was true.

CEDRIC

What did she say?

LOUISE

Nothing. She just sat back, glaring down her long
bony nose, and then skimmed the paper across the
desk at me. It fell on the floor.

CEDRIC

What did you do?

LOUISE

I left.

Silence.

CEDRIC

Well, perhaps that was the ...

LOUISE

Outside, I thought: you shitty old hag, and went back
in. She was just sitting there looking cheesed – and
even more cheesed when she saw me again.

He chuckles. She smiles briefly.

LOUISE

I sat down, crossed my knees and said: "I agree, Miss
Harper."

CEDRIC

You did?

LOUISE

She perked up then. Leaned over, like King Kong
on the skyscraper. Then I said "I am greedy. Very
greedy." She's nodding like a toy Alsatian on the
back seat of a Honda. I said: "I'm greedy to read Edith
Wharton, Wodehouse, Fitzgerald. I need all of them.
And to be supported for that, not accused of venality
for expecting education from a school. I said: "I need
these books." Picked up the list and put it on her desk.

CEDRIC

What did she say?

LOUISE

Fuck all. I left.

CEDRIC

Then what? I mean, did … ?

LOUISE

Hang on to your Y-fronts. Obviously, there'd be
no prize after that. What else would she cook up?
Anyway, it was a bit of excitement, which was good –
everything being dead boring after the exams.
People kept coming up to me for info. Anyway. It was
yesterday. The Prize Giving.

CEDRIC

Ah. Was your mother there?

LOUISE

Yup, new gear, black leather. The history teacher
found her a seat on the back row. I wish you'd been
there. Every time I came in to see you, you were
totally out of it.

CEDRIC

I know. I'm sorry. So, what happened?

LOUISE

Well, I was shoved on the front row with the rest of
the swots ...

CEDRIC

(*Smiles*) The mark of Cain.

LOUISE

And, when they got to the Lit Prize, Shitface – she'd
been giving out the books – anyway, she slithered off
sideways like an affronted locust, and Mrs Jenkins
stepped up and presented me with two lots of books
tied with pink tape.

CEDRIC

How many?

LOUISE

All of them!

CEDRIC

(*Delighted*) Really? Did she say anything?

LOUISE

What, make a speech you mean? (*She keeps him
waiting. Then smiles.*) She said: 'On behalf of the
English department, I'm proud to present the books
requested by Louise Fletcher, who has chosen not
the usual magnum opus for the bookcase, but a set
of paperbacks full of the best that writing can offer.
My colleagues and I applaud her choices ... ' Anyway,
something like that.

CEDRIC

Good. That's great. Were you pleased?

She waves him away dismissively.

LOUISE

A few people clapped. Didn't matter. Anyway, it was a good day. We went for a curry after with Mum and her new bloke.

CEDRIC

(*Interested*) Oh?

LOUISE

Yeah. He sells shower curtains. And drugs.

She pours water into a glass and a cup, gropes in his locker, laces the water with whisky, and hands him the glass. They sit back.

CEDRIC

Well ...

She leans forward, and peers into his face.

LOUISE

Are you all right?

CEDRIC

It's the lighting. We all look like cadavers.

LOUISE

Must give the visitors a shock.

CEDRIC

Never mind. (*He lifts his glass.*) Here's to ... to ...

LOUISE

To everything.

They toast each other and laugh.

Fade to black.

SCENE SIX

Cedric's Study.

CEDRIC lies on a sofa, with a rug over his knees.

CEDRIC and LOUISE have been drinking tea. He has lost weight. She has changed her hairstyle, and wears more stylish clothes. She takes his cup, puts it to one side, and sits.

> LOUISE

How've you been?

> CEDRIC

You know, I do wish people wouldn't ask that.

> LOUISE

I'm sorry.

> CEDRIC

No, I'm sorry. What else are you supposed to say?

> LOUISE

Sorry. I just . . .

> CEDRIC

It's fine. I'm fine.

> LOUISE

You're taking the . . . ?

> CEDRIC

Oh yes.

> LOUISE

No side effects?

> CEDRIC

No. Absolutely none. They're getting much more sophisticated with drugs these days.

LOUISE

Like this? (*Waves a delicate hand, turns an
aristocratic style profile.*)

CEDRIC

Not that good. Style comes next, they're still working
on that.

LOUISE

And you're feeling . . . ?

CEDRIC

Fine. Almost normal. I've been working.

He waves a hand, indicates his books and papers on the table.

LOUISE

Great. No, that's great. The drugs don't blur you off?

CEDRIC

I have them at night.

LOUISE

Nothing during the day?

CEDRIC

I can put up with that.

LOUISE

So, there is some pain?

CEDRIC

Yes, but the medication's fine. Anyway, I don't want to
work all the time. Never mind that. What about you?

LOUISE

What about me?

CEDRIC

Are you all fixed up? You've taken your time.

LOUISE

Sorry?

CEDRIC

Cambridge!

LOUISE

Oh. Yes.

CEDRIC

What college in the end?

LOUISE

What?

CEDRIC

What college? *(Silence.)* Which one? You had a choice.
(Silence.) What's the matter?

She looks at him. A long, pensive look.

CEDRIC

Don't. Have you ... ? Oh, for God's sake. You haven't.
You haven't, have you? You haven't done a runner?

LOUISE

If by that you mean have I decided to ... seek another
direction – pursue a different goal –the answer's yes.
I have.

CEDRIC

(Pause) Bugger.

LOUISE

Universities, as you knew them, don't exist anymore.
Sally – Robert's sister – supposed to be doing a
French and German degree, except she never hears
a live word of a foreign language. Tutorials? Forget

it. Sixty- plus people listening to notes from the
platform. You know as well as me ...

CEDRIC

As I.

LOUISE

As I – politicians destroyed universities to get elected
by telling everybody: 'Look, brothers and sisters,
you too can be an educated wanker with a scroll
and initials after your name.' Only they debased the
currency so much, nobody's fooled anymore.

CEDRIC

(*Silence.*) Okay. So, what will you do?

LOUISE

Take a couple of months off. Experience the relief of
not being in the wrong place.

He waits.

LOUISE

After which ...

She plays with the edge of the bedspread, then tops up his drink.
He nods thanks.

LOUISE

(*Conversationally*) I've been ... (*Clears her throat*)
I've been accepted by Guildhall.

CEDRIC

Guildhall?

LOUISE

School of Music and Drama. Drama School.

He gazes at her, stupefied.

CEDRIC

(*Puzzled*) Drama School?

LOUISE

I'm going to act.

CEDRIC

Act?

LOUISE

Yes.

CEDRIC

Act? I don't ... When did this happen ... ?

He is lost.

LOUISE

I've given it a lot of thought. Do you remember once, I was reading an Arthur Miller play, and you said read Tennessee Williams.

CEDRIC

Did I?

LOUISE

It was when you were telling me about Berlioz and musical theory. Didn't understand a word of it.

CEDRIC

You took up the flute.

LOUISE

And who begged me to stop!

They drink.

CEDRIC

Act?

She nods.

CEDRIC

You want to act? Read, learn, quote and requote other people's thoughts?

LOUISE

(*Shrugs*) Well, yes. Shakespeare. Chekhov. I may end up directing. Or I could be a writer. I mean, it's hard for women having to settle for displacement activities like men, now we're released from the holy miracle of bearing and nourishing children.

CEDRIC

(*Confused*) What?

LOUISE

Well, it was all so hand-held. Can't have that. Yeah, a writer. Sounds okay.

CEDRIC

(*Dry*) All settled then.

LOUISE

You never know. I could be the next Lillian Hellman. Should be okay with the right gear. Saggy cardigan, side parting (*pointing at her hair*) with a slide, and my entourage . . .

He frowns, puzzled

LOUISE

. . . theatre fans, terrorists, clubbers – Tasmanians of course.

CEDRIC

What the <u>hell</u> are you talking about?

LOUISE

No, you're right. Fuck all that. It's the boards for me.

CEDRIC

Are you serious?

LOUISE

Yuh.

CEDRIC

You want to be an actress?

LOUISE

It is now accepted as a respectable calling.

CEDRIC

But you've never shown any particular ... I mean you read plays. You read everything but ...

LOUISE

I played Hedda last year.

CEDRIC

Only because the tall girl fell off her bike.

LOUISE

People said I was better.

CEDRIC

No, they didn't. You played her for laughs.

LOUISE

What was I supposed to do? Torvald standing there like a jammy twat ...

CEDRIC

He was stunned by what you were doing. I'm surprised you weren't arrested for that bed scene with the judge. That's not in the text.

LOUISE

Spiritually it is.

He looks at her drily. She smiles, giving in. He looks at her
reflectively.

                    CEDRIC
You really mean it? Acting?

She nods.

                    CEDRIC
Why?

                    LOUISE
Because I want a life with life in it.

                    CEDRIC
By inhabiting fiction.

                    LOUISE
And you prefer fact?

                    CEDRIC
Yes. Facts are the building blocks. The bricks we use
to build our world.

                    LOUISE
(Into his face) What about all your talk about
imagination? Anyway, I want insecurity.

                    CEDRIC
(Laughs) Why?

                    LOUISE
What's the alternative? Some dead funk-hole of a
life? I've thought about it a lot. Imagined myself here.
There. In a uniform. Indoors. Outdoors. Abroad. But
doing what? Research, teaching, something arty,
designing, printing, publishing ... selling?

CEDRIC

What about good works? Amnesty – Médecins Sans
Frontières? You've got the bottle for it.

LOUISE

But not the vocation. *(Slight pause.)* When I told you I
was going to Norfolk to ski ...

CEDRIC

(Waves a hand) I thought you were pulling my leg for
being nosy.

LOUISE

(Chuckles.) I went to see a woman in Norfolk. Sister
Marie-Thérèse. I stayed overnight at a nunnery.

CEDRIC

What for?

LOUISE

Advice. She told me to leave nunning to people who
had a vocation for it, like her. She suggested politics.

CEDRIC

Politics?

LOUISE

I thought about it but, oh Christ, all those ball-
breaking non-achieving meetings – worse than
stacking shelves. At least that's physical exercise.
Democracy's crap. Benevolent despotism's the only
thing that works.

CEDRIC

Yes, you'd be good at it.

LOUISE

No. So, will you be watching my Rosalind or not? I'll
want notes. I'll need plenty. You're going to have to sit
on the end of Row F, fixture. I'll get you tickets.

CEDRIC

What about my low boredom threshold?

LOUISE

I'll fix that. When you're in, I'll figure out a coup de
theatre. "Adam, who is that girl on the swing playing
with her minge?" (She sighs heavily.)

CEDRIC

Now what?

LOUISE

What's the use of dreaming up a stage name when you
have to screw an ugly old man with grey pubic hair
just to get a good part?

CEDRIC

I thought you said you didn't go in for all that.

LOUISE

I don't, but this is business. It's okay. You just close
your eyes and think of Brad Pitt. It's what he's for.

A heavy pause.

CEDRIC

(At last) I do know a couple of people.

LOUISE

(Quick) Who?

CEDRIC

A London producer. I wrote his essays at Oxford. And
his son's.

LOUISE
And the other one?

CEDRIC
A New York Mr Big.

LOUISE
Excellent. Be there. Row F every performance. And
don't turn into one of those old farts who falls asleep
and then goes like this. (*She does a waking up and
snorting fit.*)

CEDRIC
Oh, they're just theatregoers' husbands. Anyway,
by the time you get employment, I'll have probably
kicked the bucket. How long is your course?

LOUISE
Two years. That okay?

CEDRIC
Yeah, I should think so. Possibly.

LOUISE
What have they said?

He shrugs.

LOUISE
They were going to tell you.

CEDRIC
Yes.

LOUISE
We'll have they?

CEDRIC
In a manner of speaking – no.

LOUISE

What's that supposed to mean?

CEDRIC

Diagnosis is a mug's game. Why lose points by getting
it wrong?

LOUISE

So, they weren't specific. Didn't tell you how long
you'd got. Did they at least say whether it was years –
months ... ?

CEDRIC

They're not supposed to do that. Although, they do it
all the time. Only God knows when you're going to die.

LOUISE

You're getting me worried.

CEDRIC

Don't be.

LOUISE

You'd better not die. Think what you'd be missing.

CEDRIC

(Dramatically) God yes! (Back of hand to brow.)
Spine-destroying seats at the Bush ... theatre run
by the politically correct Oxbridge mafia on our tax
money. I don't envy you.

LOUISE

Have you finished?

CEDRIC

No. Aim low, darling. Television. Try for a quiet soap.
Rural background. Nice-looking women with low

voices. One I can watch with a malt and the Times crossword. Not too late at night, okay?

LOUISE

Piss off. You love the theatre. You've told me. Hurtling down the M1 for all the greats I've missed. Edith Evans, Wolfit, O'Toole, Sir John, Sir Laurence. You won't need to stick around for my pathetic contribution.

CEDRIC

You'll be off the hook. Think of that moment of calm as they call the half. "At least <u>he</u>'s not sitting out there totting up the waste of time and money to get to bloody Row F." (*Slight pause*) Well, if I linger on long enough I may come across you accidentally.

LOUISE

Oh, very supportive.

CEDRIC

Support? You want support? If you need that give up now.

She turns, open-mouthed at his coldness.

CEDRIC

And that is the best support you'll ever receive. File it. Stow it away. Remember it as you lurch to your auditions.

LOUISE

Lurch – yah. I'm aware of the knock-knees.

CEDRIC

Where do you think the John Wayne walk came from? Didn't hold <u>him</u> back. Nope. On your own. Solo. Forget support.

LOUISE

(*Sarcastic*) Thank you.

Slight pause.

CEDRIC

We've been ... apart from, I hope, friends ...

She turns to him in surprise.

LOUISE

Of course!

CEDRIC

... a satisfactorily profitable mutual investment. Now it's time to move on.

As she tries to speak.

CEDRIC

You'll be taking me with you. I'll fade as time goes on, but trace elements will remain. What you need will be there. We don't have to inhabit the same space for that.

LOUISE

Fine. I'm not asking for consolation. (*Clears her throat at last.*) If you're not going to support me – if you aren't going to support me, where will you be?

CEDRIC

Where will I be?

He hoists himself up, then shrugs, lifting his hands in a 'Who knows' gesture.

LOUISE

That's all very well.

CEDRIC

It's all you're getting.

LOUISE

Thanks a lot.

CEDRIC

You'll be fine.

LOUISE

You think so?

She moves about, touching things restlessly. Looks over at him moodily.

CEDRIC

Just believe in yourself. Adamantly – mineral hard.
And be close to tears at the same time.

LOUISE

I see. Dead easy.

CEDRIC

Not difficult. You simply relate at all times, with
every phrase, to the relevant human response. With
accuracy and the correct tone.

LOUISE

Tell the truth, you mean.

He smiles, delighted with her.

CEDRIC

It's why theatre – real theatre – live theatre – is
so important. It matters because occasionally –
unexpectedly – something happens. Takes place.
Things change. You see it in their faces – the
audiences – as they come down the steps. Oh, don't
worry. It doesn't happen that often. We couldn't deal

with it if it did. It's why we need the reassurance of sentiment to get through the day. Can't expect all to be solved in the second act. (*Slight pause*) Sorry, it's the whisky talking.

LOUISE

No, it isn't. (*Pause.*) What I want to know is ... What I want to know is: where you'll be. Where will you be?

CEDRIC

How the hell should I know? I'm a scientist, I work with data.

LOUISE

(*Shakes her head*) Uh-uhn. You're one of the five best scientists in the world. You lot work on hunches. You've told me. What's your hunch – angels' wings – fires of retribution – sweet fat nothing? You must have some idea. Some conclusions.

CEDRIC

Conclusions? (*Scratches his eyebrow.*) Yes. One.

LOUISE

One?

CEDRIC

A good one. Reassuring ... intriguing.

LOUISE

One? Okay, what?

CEDRIC

We don't know anything.

LOUISE

Thanks very much.

CEDRIC

What we know ... what we know is what we are
equipped to know. Think about it. A dog has
immeasurably superior sense perception compared
to humans. Books full of verified anecdotes. Animals
aware of impending death, arrivals, disasters. I had
a terrier – Dodger. He quit whatever he was up to
the moment I left the lab. Waited at the gate until I
got home. We timed him. He couldn't have heard me
leaving the lab. I was two miles away.

LOUISE

(*Suddenly depressed*) If you die, who am I going to
talk to?

She looks at him gloomily.

CEDRIC

Well, there's always yourself.

LOUISE

I spend my life talking to myself.

CEDRIC

And anybody else who takes your fancy.

LOUISE

I'll have to go on the hunt for ...

CEDRIC

It happens naturally. In between there are cats, dogs.
Trees are good – and the sky – the English sky on a
good day. Birds. Skylarks. Owls ...

LOUISE

Owls?

CEDRIC

No, not owls, blundering great idiots. Try firebirds.
More your style.

She looks down at him with genial condescension.

LOUISE

Daft. Tea?

CEDRIC

Okay.

She exits.

CEDRIC

(*Calls*) Could I have some bread and butter?

He lies back against the pillows.

Pause.

CEDRIC

(*Quietly*) God I'm tired.

A long pause.

We realise that the man has left us.

LOUISE enters backwards, manhandling a tea-tray. She
approaches the bed.

LOUISE

I brought you some biscuits.

She pours the tea, and hands him the mug. There is no response.

She leans, inspecting his averted face.

LOUISE

D'you want it or not? Oh well.

She puts the mug back on the tray and turns towards the exit.

She stops, drops the tray, and turns back to the bed.

LOUISE

Cedric? *(Quietly)* Cedric? Cedric, it's Louise.

She stands over him, gazing down for a still moment.

She moves away, indecisive, then flicks a look back at the bed, and slumps into a chair.

LOUISE

(Quietly, to herself) Oh bugger.

Fade to black.

The End.

MY WARREN

for Janet Henfry

MY WARREN was first presented on the 5th of March, 1973, by *Inter-Action* and the *Women's Theatre Group* at the Almost Free Theatre, starring JANET HENFREY, and directed by SUE PARRISH.

Stage Manager	NICK BURGE
ASM	LAUREL-JANA MARKS
Lighting Design	PETER SOUTHCOTT

In 1979, it was revived by the King's Head Theatre, Islington, where it ran from April 23rd to May 5th.

CAST

Eileen	JANET HENFREY
Directed by	SUE PARRISH
Stage Manager	PHILIPPA MOUNTAIN

MY WARREN

Street noises.

The sound of a key in the lock. A door opens and closes. The sound of a canary singing.

>EILEEN
>
>*(Arriving, tired)* Placido, shut up. Ooh! *(Sounds as she unpacks shopping.)* The trouble with Safeways is you keep seeing things. Salmon quiche! I mean! And there's enough for four. It won't keep. It'll go all fridgey.
>Next door's cat again.
>She keeps telling me off.
>He's not fat!
>Kettle. Kettle … kettle …

Sound of kettle.

Chink of teacup and spoon.

>EILEEN
>
>Lemon … lemon … lemon.

Sounds as she makes her mug of tea.

>EILEEN
>
>*(Sits)* Ahh. That's better. Ooh! So bloody hot without milk! Never mind, Eileen. Cholesterol.

She sips.

>EILEEN
>
>You must eat.

There's nothing wrong he says.

It's stress.

Tablets made me cross-eyed. Stupid fool of a doctor.

If he clipped Placido's claws, he'd have his foot off.

It could be an ulcer.

Or a lump.

No. (*Puts down the cup.*) Bloody man's right for once.

It's tension.

Damned copier on, day after day. Right through your head! Headache Dispenser, Mark One.

<u>They</u> don't even notice it. Too busy yelling. No wonder I'm not hungry!

<u>He'd</u> eat donkey's bum so long as the menu was in French.

Eat anything.

What must it be like to have an appetite?

Must be like feeling young all the time.

A bit of fruit. No, you'll get the runs again. Ohh, you cunning little devil – you know what you're after! Ginger biscuit!

Sound of chair as she rises.

Crackle as she opens the packet of biscuits. She eats.

EILEEN

Mmm. Oh, go on, have two.

That's better.

Pause.

EILEEN

Oh dear.

Here. None of that. Steady as you go. Come on now ...
Oh God ... oh God, oh God please help me. I don't like it. It won't stop. I can't, and it frightens me.

I want to push a knitting needle in her face, in her
eye, I want to kill her.
It's this voice ... telling me. No, I won't!
I won't!
(*Groans*) Ohhh ...

Crackle of the biscuit packet. She eats and talks at the same time.

> EILEEN

I ca ...

She groans and quietly, subsides.

> EILEEN

All right, Eileen.
You're all right.
You'll be okay in a minute.

She breathes deeply several times.

> EILEEN

Okay now ... Watch your programme.

She switches on the TELEVISION, and changes programme from
loud pop, to US soap, to programme on motor racing, programme
on chat presenter showing off, to rap.

> EILEEN

(*Savagely*) Oh great. (*Switches off.*) There must be
something.

Sound of paper as she looks at the Radio Times.

> EILEEN

Cooking ...
Makeover ...
Your garden glamorised in a day. Cooking. Incest ...
Well, I'll mark that.

Ooh, my hip! That <u>fool</u> of a doctor. It's no good, I'll have to go back.

She groans, the chair creaks as she sits.

EILEEN

Bloody doctors.

You can see it in their eyes.

"Here she comes – Miss Frigidaire – spinster of the year."

Couldn't even get herself a man.

Not one.

Ever.

Not even a grope.

A cuddle.

A shove-up against the wall.

Zilch.

Nothing.

Zero.

Why didn't you make a fool of yourself like the rest of them? Who do you think you are?

You should have used make-up. Done all the silliness.

That's what they wanted – what they went after.

You weren't that bad. Better than a lot of them.

Nice thin legs.

But oh no.

(*Mimics herself.*) "I want to be loved for myself."

Doesn't bloody work that way, mate.

She laughs, grimly.

There was just the once.

Nearly.

Face like a bum.

I thought, oh you poor bugger.

I wouldn't have wasted all that time with him if he
hadn't been so awful.
Listening to that voice.
Eating curry.
Then he goes off and marries a dwarf.
I should have settled for him. I could have shut my
eyes shut and pretended it was Bruce Willis.

She strikes a match, lights up, draws on her cigarette, and exhales
with pleasure.

Eleven years.
Eleven years we'd have been married.
Three children – Rachel – Jake – little Davy.
Oh, what must it be like? Ecstasy.
That's what I've missed … ecstasy.
They're getting it all right. If he's not with his wife, or
that Belgian piece, he's with her, the dirty devil.
And Rob and Maggie in Sales, and now Josie with
Brian.
Why couldn't I have met a nice boy like that? Falls
into her lap at nineteen, lovely boy like that.
Ohh! They ought to pay people to cuddle you.
If they gave it on the National Health, there wouldn't
be nearly so many stoppages.
Put that out and stop buying them!

She crushes the cigarette out onto a saucer.

EILEEN

I wouldn't mind if they left it alone.
We're supposed to be there to work. God knows what
would happen if I wasn't running that office – it would
collapse. At least I've got the satisfaction of knowing.
Oh, balls to that, Eileen!

You're getting as coarse as the rest of them.
There's no romance!
No sensitivity!
The way they ... it makes you ashamed to be a
woman.
Treating me like a gauleiter.
I'd love a chat now and then about clothes ... hair.
I'm no different because I'm older.

Her chair scrapes as she gets up, and looks in the glass.

EILEEN

You know, you could look ten years younger. Write
to that magazine. Get them to do a transformation.
What is it they call it? Makeover. They've done
women worse than you.
Oh Christ. I've forgotten again.

She moves chairs.

EILEEN

Right.
Breathe in ...

She breathes in and out deeply.

EILEEN

Left right, left right – three four ...
Now relax. It's no good if you don't relax. You could
(*Pants with effort.*) join a club.
Like that woman.
(*Panting.*) Signed up all the clubs where she'd meet
men.
Snooker. Golf. Rifle club.
Even (*puff*) bloody fishing.
It worked.

Even if it did end in divorce, she got a kid.
(*Puffs*) Get out and meet people.
Stay stuck in here, who's going to come up five flights
to winkle you out?
Get your skates on. Take a chance on life.

Slight pause.

I offered to babysit ... ooh this shoulder's stiff. I
suppose they didn't want to be beholden.
It's since she came.
Completely different atmosphere.
I've always taken him his tea. I know how he likes it.
Full-cream and infused properly. Gnats' pee the way
she does it.
I'm not telling her.
It was me found the laundry for his shirts.
Oh, I wish we were back in the old days.
One office, all mail order. I didn't mind the stairs.
We made that place.
I never begrudged a minute of the extra time. It was
exciting.
He's not like his father. He never forgot. A bunch of
anemones every birthday – even tulips once.
They sit there, painting their nails, changing the
subject when I walk through the door.
It's very ... You'd think I was something the cat
brought in. (*She assumes a simpering male voice.*)
"Ew, we don't talk about problem and solution now,
Miss Arnold, it's all challenge and response ... "
Giggle, giggle, giggle.
Oh, I've stopped.
A few more stretchy ones, then on the floor with you,
Eileen. Where's the yoga book?

No, that's enough. They all get arthritis, athletes. You
don't want to overdo it.
That's your story. (*Laughs at herself.*)
Now.
Let's see.
Done the ironing ...
I'll keep my book for tonight, or I won't have anything
to read.
I could tidy my drawers.
Oh, it's all so <u>silly</u>!
Why should I have to live like this?
Nobody should. Staying in fifty weeks a year to
scrape enough for two weeks off. It's not worth it!
What chance have you got? Woman on your own they
see you coming.
I know!
I haven't put my lovely big wooden button on my
sweater!

She opens a drawer, and takes out her newly knitted sweater.
Grunts as she tries it on.

EILEEN

Slip you on ...
Now. Let's see how we look.
Ooh. Now that ... mmm ... mohair ...
I knew the dark mauve was right. Every time I sew
up, I think that's it – no more knitting. I won't do
another one. You're not an old lady yet. (*She laughs.*)
Come on, you know you've got your eye on that
bronzy brown wool!
Keep passing the shop.
Oh, walk the other way home!

How do you think you're going to get to Spain if you
spend, spend, spend?!
Never know, I might have my veins done by then.
I must be near the top after three years. Then I could
walk and walk!
Spain!

She clicks her fingers, singing a bit of the *Habanera* from *Carmen*.

EILEEN

I like Spain.
Quieter than Italy.
More reserved.
And cheaper.
These welts could have done with another inch.
Pity about the bullfighting.
Mmm. Serves you right for following a pattern. Better
when you work it out for yourself.
Still – not bad.
Perhaps I'll just pop out for a breath of air. Give you a
little outing. Good idea.
Bag ... bag ...
Coat ...
Yes, it looks great, that stand-up collar. Right ...
You turd.
You rat.
Off to the bloody pictures – that's what you were up
to!
And welsh rarebit and a pot of tea after!
Who do you think's going to look at you, you bloody
twerp.
Bloody stand-up collar and all ...
Get your coat off.
Now.

You've got your books.

You've got your television . . . your radio.

You're as greedy as the rest of them – and cunning
with it.

Honestly, you'd fritter the lot.

Make up your <u>mind</u>!

Do you want to go on holiday, or don't you?

She sits.

EILEEN

I must have a holiday.

Something to look forward to.

Otherwise I can't . . .

If only Serie A wasn't on so late. If I try to video Inter
or Lazio, I get some porn film.

Such lovely, lovely men.

Zidane.

The Insaghis . . . Pippo and Simeone.

Little Raul. Rivaldo.

Del Piero! Alessandro! Face off a Renaissance
painting.

And Figo.

Luis Figo.

Portuguese.

Frightening. A frown like Michelangelo's David.

Figo.

I could just go out for a walk.

Not take my purse.

You might feel bad. Have to take a taxi. Get one of
your panics.

Oh, I feel rough!

Why? Why do I feel so rotten all the time?

Maybe if I had more guts ... It's so sore – right across
here. Right across the liver.
The area of firm decision – that's what the Chinks call
it.
"How's life?"
"Depends upon the liver!"
Toughen up.
Stand up to them.
Look at Madonna!
Joan Collins!
Barry Manilow! Try and put him down, he just
smiles.
I should have gone on that course with Phyllis
Barnes.
Her own shop now.
And you can stop feeling jealous and polish that fire
surround before it grows a fur coat.

She gets out the brasso and rags. Groans as she gets down.

EILEEN

Right, fender.
You're going to get it.

She rubs, humming *Putting on the Ritz*.

EILEEN

Putting on the Ritz!
Dada da dada da da da dooper ...
Trying hard to look like Gary Cooper, super-duper!
That leather seat could do with some beeswax.
Funny the way soldiers spit on their boots to get a
shine.
You don't have to be that shiny. It's repellent.

Rubs, humming.

EILEEN

(Snarls suddenly) Macrobiotic food!
He sits there nodding, never gone hungry in his life.
And I should know. I do his credit cards.
Of course she can live on lemongrass when he's
treating her to fillet steak and salmon three times a
week.
I've a good mind to drop a word in Elaine's ear, there
are those little girls to think of.
Stop it Eileen.
Jealous and you know it.
I wish it was me.
Why didn't I play daft and helpless like the rest of
them, instead of working my ass off?
Why didn't I giggle … laugh at the jokes … show off
my tits?
You have to play your cards.
I should have pretended.
Been cunning, like Odysseus.
Worn red.
Nobody ever noticed you.
I hate them.
All of them.
I hate the lot of them.
No, you don't.
Pull yourself together.
And watch your back.
They'll have you out of it.
I've seen him looking for a way to pay me off – then
remembering what a bargain I am.
If only they'd pull their weight!
Mad panic by Wednesday, nightmare Thursday … by
Friday, I think I can't go through this one more week!

We're understaffed!
No – not if they worked, if they pulled their weight.
If anything, we're overstaffed.
Just remember: they'll have you out.
Don't give them an excuse.
Be pleasant . . . friendly.
If you can't like them for themselves, pretend they're
somebody else.
Somebody lively like Liz Hurley.
Or Joanna Lumley.
She'd be there in a crisis.
Sue Lawley should let you choose a favourite chap
to take on the Island. Wow! That wonderful Ian
Bostridge who looks like young Lochinvar. I'd knit for
him!
Thomas Allen?
Bryan Terfel?
Lovely voices echoing off the trees!
Gerard Depardieu – oh, he's the one.
He'd get the vines growing, and pull the flotsam off
the beach, and make salads out of sorrel and garlic.
Oooh . . . vive la France!
Yeah?
Trouble is your imagination goes too far, Eileen.
Be reasonable.
Stay in the ball park. Young Jeff could be Keanu
Reeves. He's got the twinkle for it. I could pretend
Josie's my favourite niece that I have to look out for.
Well, you do that anyway. All she does is misfile.
And what about Messalina?
Eileen – cut it out.
Whether you like it or not, she's part of the team.

Enough bad feeling already – if you don't nip it in the
bud . . . She's as weak as piss.
Just when you think you're safe – out.
I wouldn't get placed easily. Not now.
Watch out for yourself, my dear.
Suck up to the little snake.
Why should I?
Why should I have to?
Listen to rubbish hour after hour – and if it isn't about
her, is she listening? Is she hell.
That's it.
Flattery.
Tell her she's gorgeous. Puts Catherine Zeta Jones
in the shade. Best legs in the business. Great hair.
Lovely eyes. Amazing bloody beauty spot.
And listen!
Nod and smile. Look dazzled. I can shut my mind off.
It's the same drivel every day. All you have to do is
say 'Ooh, wonderful!' Nothing to it.
After all, she is pretty.
She is a pretty girl.

She groans.

I knew there'd be trouble when she came for the
interview.
Funny. I thought it would be Mr Lionel – not him.
I keep thinking they're laughing at me!
Stop poisoning yourself, Eileen.
Keep thinking she's threatening me. It's got to stop,
It's paranoia. No more bad thoughts.
They're a bunch of kids. You can't expect them to
have your experience. Loyalty to the job. Let's face it,
none of us would be doing it by choice.

Get a healthier attitude.

You're the senior. It's up to you to create the

ambience. Set the pace.

Be encouraging, not critical. Lead by example.

Lay back. Good grief, I don't suppose one of them

gives me a thought once they're out of that door, little

devils.

A KNOCK on the door.

Hullo! *(Going)* Who on earth can that be?

She exits.

EILEEN

(Voice distant) Sorry? Oh, thank you for bringing it

in. Thank you. Sorry you've been troubled, I'm not

expecting anything. Thank you.

She returns.

EILEEN

Some wretched free gift I suppose. Well, it goes

straight back without a stamp.

The thing is not to get bitter.

Keep going. They've made a good job of this wrap. I

must show it to Packaging.

If there is bad feeling ... ask yourself Eileen. Is it you?

Being on your own you imagine so much. *(She*

unwraps the package.) What on earth's this?

There must be some mistake.

Where's the leaflet? It looks like some sort of ...

She takes out a dildo-vibrator.

EILEEN

(Gasps deeply.) Oh!

She sits.

                    EILEEN

Their idea of a joke, I suppose.

Now hold on.

Breathe deep. In ... out ... in ... out ... in ...

Oh God!

So much for good will.

You bloody fool. When will you learn?

Oh God.

You know. You know what they are. Never a day
without spite. Oh, they'll have had fun dreaming this
up.

But she breaks down.

                    EILEEN

So mean! (*She cries.*) Come on. You've got your flat.
You've got your telly, for God's sake! (*She cries.*)
You're <u>not</u> lonely. You've got the library. The whole
of the world's literature down the road. You're not
starving. There's the park. There's your holiday ...
your holi ... you've got ...

But she sobs.

                    EILEEN

Oh, I don't want it ... I don't like it! Please, I can't bear
it any more. I don't want it. You have to be so brave all
the time on your own. I'm tired. I can't go on fighting.
I fight every day. I don't give in to it. I keep on. I don't
give up – but I'm tired!

I want to go to bed.

I don't want to wake up any more (*She cries.*)

I don't want to wash ...

I don't want to do my teeth ...

I don't want to get dressed any more ...

I want to stay in bed.

Please God …

(Shuddering sobs.) The food churns up inside …

I can't stand the noise of the traffic …

You get pushed about on the tube … … . .

I'm frightened!

I can't even go in the lift. I'm too frightened!

I don't want to go there anymore.

Please God, don't make me!

They hate me.

Silence.

What a joke.

All that stuff about God.

He's not there.

What do they want to tell you all that for? (She

sniffs.) Oh, now look what you've done. You'll have to

wash that. Can't have a snotty cushion.

She tries to laugh, but it ends in a sigh.

It's bad.

Monday morning! How can I … ?

Tablets.

She opens a drawer, takes out some tablets, and gets a glass of
water.

There.

I'll take two more tonight, that should black me out.

Rustle of paper as she inspects the gift.

What a waste of money.

They've got it to burn. I wish I had the money to play

filthy jokes!

It was her.

Oh, it was her.

They'll all have joined in. They'll have had a good
laugh – but we know whose idea it was. She never
leaves it alone!
Stupid waste.
I wonder if I could take it back.
You <u>would</u> have to tear the box, Eileen.
That would do them in and turn the tables. Talk about
the last laugh.
I've half a mind to do it.
I know where they bought it. They never stop about
the place.
Marital aids!
You wouldn't have the nerve to go through the door.
Probably want me to take a credit note. Exchange it
for a thong.
Forget it. Forget it, Eileen.
What a shame.
What a shame. I bet they aren't cheap.

Rustle of paper as she looks for the price.

EILEEN

Oh, batteries and all!

She puts the batteries in the dildo.

EILEEN

So, you put . . . Oh! (*Jumps at the sound of the
vibrator.*)
Well I never.
They've made it a good size. Value for money. Mmm.
(*Switches it off.*)
Good grief. Imagine going about with all that stuck on
the front of you.
I suppose you get used to it.

Weird though. "If I were crested, not cloven."
Wonderful woman, Queen Elizabeth. Cate Blanchett
had a good stab at her.
Being Australian helps, I daresay.

She turns on the television. SOUND of MAURICE JARRE MUSIC.

> EILEEN
>
> Oh Christ, it's Lawrence of Arabia!
> Ahh! Stunning! Never mind the music, Eileen ... the
> desert! Oh, it makes you feel ... and Peter O'Toole ...
> magic!

MUSIC.

> EILEEN
>
> What a useless thing.
> Honestly, I do hate waste.

She turns on the vibrator.

> EILEEN
>
> I wonder how long the battery lasts.
> Wonderful desert ......

Sound of vibrator, louder, against the music.

> EILEEN
>
> Oh, Peter ...
> *(Squeals.)* Ooh!
> Ah! Peter!
> Well I never! ...

MUSIC increase in volume.

> EILEEN
>
> Oh. Eileen ...
> Peter!
> Oh!

Oh, Eileen!!! Eileen!!
Ahh!!!!

MUSIC – loud.

Fade to black.

The End.

Other plays by – or adapted by – Pam Gems currently in print:

CAMILLE	(Bloomsbury)
DUSA, FISH, STAS and VI	(Bloomsbury)
MARLENE	(Bloomsbury)
MRS PAT	(Bloomsbury)
PIAF	(Bloomsbury)
QUEEN CHRISTINA	(Bloomsbury)
THE LADY FROM THE SEA	(Bloomsbury)
THE LITTLE MERMAID	(Bloomsbury)
THE SNOW PALACE	(Bloomsbury)
YERMA	(Bloomsbury)
STANLEY	(Nick Hern Books)
THE SEAGULL	(Nick Hern Books)
UNCLE VANYA	(Nick Hern Books)
THE CHERRY ORCHARD	(Cambridge University Press)

Bloomsbury
www.bloomsbury.com

Nick Hern Books
www.nickhernbooks.co.uk

Cambridge University Press
www.cambridge.org

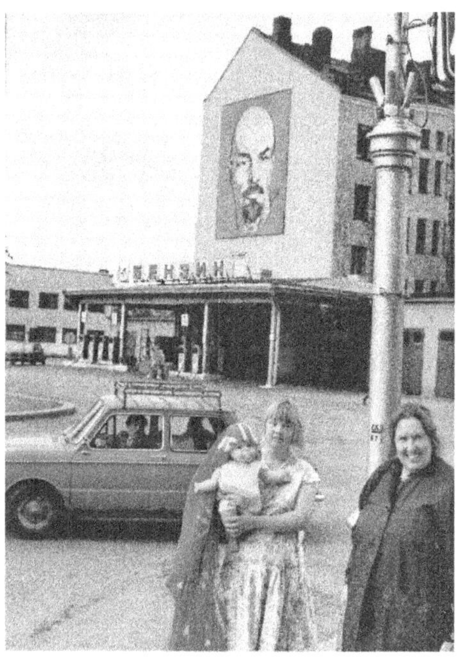

Pam Gems and her daughter, Lala, in the Soviet Union, 1986.

Q

website: www.quotabooks.com

email: info@quotabooks.com

Twitter: @Quotabooks